# Scattered Raindrops

✦

## Reflections on the Word

*Deacon Bill Rich*

iUniverse, Inc.
New York  Lincoln  Shanghai

# Scattered Raindrops
## Reflections on the Word

iUniverse, Inc.

For information address:
iUniverse, Inc.
2021 Pine Lake Road, Suite 100
Lincoln, NE 68512
www.iuniverse.com

ISBN: 0-595-33164-5

Printed in the United States of America

Thus says the LORD:
  Just as from the heavens
  the rain and snow come down
and do not return there
  till they have watered the earth,
  making it fertile and fruitful,
giving seed to the one who sows
  and bread to the one who eats,
so shall my word be
  that goes forth from my mouth;
my word shall not return to me void,
  but shall do my will,
  achieving the end for which I sent it.

*—Isaiah 55: 10-11*

# *Contents*

## FALL

# *Preface*

Other than getting married, the most transforming experience in my life was becoming a Permanent Deacon in the Roman Catholic Church. The decision took almost six years of discussion with my wife Frannie and our children, a good deal of prayer and, in the end, a willingness to trust. The three years of formal training leading up to my ordination seemed to fly by, although I am sure it was a very challenging time for my family. I loved the classes, particularly those devoted to scripture, and felt like a whole new world was opening up to me.

During the second year of our training, one of our classes was called "Homiletics"—the giving of homilies. Our teacher opened the class with the statement, "Preaching is the primary way most people are touched by their minister." I decided this must be true, and I committed myself to three ideas taught in that class: never give a homily unless you are fully prepared (including an outline); always preach what you personally believe; and do as Jesus did: proclaim the Good News.

Since then, I have struggled with these guidelines at times, but have never forgotten them. They forced me to read, reflect, observe, and pray. I love to preach and was soon doing it whenever I could, whether at Masses or on retreats or in bible study seminars. Over time, a set of convictions emerged. These convictions form the basis for this book.

Our tendency to focus on the divinity of Jesus creates the potential for missing His primary message. Jesus did not think of Himself as a theologian or the founder of a church. Jesus saw Himself as God's messenger, sent to impart practical wisdom on how to live this life to the fullest, in preparation for union with the Divine in the next. Jesus spoke about the ordinary things in our lives, things like priorities, choices, faith, hope, fear, and forgiveness. He spoke about ordinary things because that is where the divine is found. He called His followers to commit themselves to the presence of the divine in their lives, promising a serenity and peace He called happiness to those willing to love as the divine loved them. In a very real sense, He died so that we might live.

Several years ago, a young friend of mine suggested I publish a book of my homilies. For reasons I can no longer remember, I decided he had a good idea. It may have had something to do with the fact that my cancer had just resurfaced. It may have been because similar suggestions had been made by other acquaintances. It may have been simply my compulsive nature.

The name *Scattered Raindrops* occurred to me for two reasons. "Raindrops" comes from one of my favorite scripture passages, Isaiah 55:10-11, with its metaphor of rain and snow representing God's promise of proactive involvement in our lives.

"Scattered" refers to the fact that the reflections included in this book do not represent any preplanning on my part. They appear in chronological order (with one small exception), based on the church year, which begins with Advent in early December. The only criteria for inclusion was that someone asked if the homily I had just given would ever be written down.

In the process of writing, rewriting, and editing, it became apparent that homilies as given have inherent disadvantages when one attempts to use them in a book. Most notable is reference to scripture passages without repeating, or even giving their source. The reason for this is obvious, as a homily is given right after the scripture passages have been read. Addressing this issue led me to drop the term "homily" and replace it with "reflection" whenever discussing the contents of this book.

I would like to thank Amy Berrier and Anna Chapman for their important help in editing my work. Most people need only one guardian angel, but I required two. My thanks also to Don Gray, who inspired my original fascination with scripture as a professor in my training to become a Deacon. He was infinitely patient with my endless questions and assertions then, and has periodically provided much needed guidance and counsel over the years. I particularly appreciate his suggestions concerning the reflections in this book. Finally, I want to thank my wife, who was invaluable in her willingness to review my work, act as a sounding board for ideas, and put up with my many mood swings as I struggled to find my way.

Recently, someone asked me whether I thought there was any market for this book. I responded by saying I had no idea beyond the twelve I planned to buy as Christmas presents. Having thought about that answer, I think I would like to add one closing thought: I hope anyone who does happen to read this book receives just a small portion of what I gained from the writing. Truly, when we make the effort to give, we do receive more than we have given.

Deacon Bill Rich
The Red House
Tamworth, NH
September 2004

# Winter

# *Repentance*

It is easy to misunderstand repentance. For many, it evokes images of giving up theoretically wrong, but enjoyable activities, whatever they may be, for some altruistic but lackluster existence. In actuality, the word means something very different. Repentance involves deciding what is important to us.

Most of us spend little time thinking about what is important. I am not sure why. Perhaps we feel we are too busy. Perhaps we are part of the vast majority who operate mindlessly on the principle that the accumulation of material wealth is the only thing that matters. Perhaps, deep down, we don't think such reflection will accomplish anything. But it does.

Almost without exception, doing what is important to us produces a sense of enduring happiness, usually because it helps us feel good about ourselves. Knowing what is important to us allows us to spend more time on what makes us happy. If we don't decide what's important, someone else will. And that, at best, is a chancy proposition.

Repentance is a two-step process. First, one must discern the rough ways: the mountains and winding roads in our lives—activities, people, or thought patterns—that rob us of our serenity by abusing our sense of self-worth. Think of it as taking off your robe of misery, however big or small it may be. It can be as obvious as an unfulfilling job, as difficult as an abusive relationship, or as subtle as feeling not good enough. For years, a friend of mine assumed that she had to agree with everything her husband said. A period of reflection helped her to understand that subservience in any intimate relationship precludes the nurturing growth required for happiness.

The second half of repentance involves dedicating ourselves to what lifts us up, to what helps us live more fully; doing something we have always wanted, but never dared, to do; taking time to right a relationship gone wrong; listening to music that touches the soul. Try, and you will be surprised by the result. As Paul says, "This is my prayer: that your love increase ever more and more in knowledge and every kind of perception, to discern what is of value…" (Philippians 1:9)

Repentance involves ridding ourselves of the cluttered garbage in our lives and replacing it with those things that provide enduring happiness. Joseph Campbell, a well-known scholar who spent his life studying comparative religions, said it well when he stated, "The Divine is always calling us to 'follow our bliss.'" Sometimes it is hard for us to accept this reality, but think of how much better life could be if we only would.

When the rush of the Christmas holiday season starts, almost all of us have an endless list of things to do: send cards, hang decorations, erect a tree, buy gifts, make ready for family visitors. The focus is on others, on things, and on things for others. The call to repentance is a call to focus instead on the gift that is you.

Repentance is always helpful, but it is particularly important in Advent, the time of year when we celebrate the coming of Jesus. We celebrate His coming not as judge, king, or critic, but as a child. Christmas is a time when Jesus can be born again in you and me, if we let Him. The process of repentance helps ensure that this year there will be room for Him in our inn.

"Prepare the way of the LORD," says Isaiah. (Isaiah 40:3) But how? What are some practical ways to prepare the gift that is you?

I can think of no better way to discard what weighs us down than by sharing the problems of our life with another person, particularly if we can muster the courage to share the failings that we promised ourselves we would never tell anyone. This basic step can be incredibly freeing. There is something about the process of sharing our wrongs with someone else that helps us let go of the accumulated emotional waste in our lives. In addition, it is often surprising to realize how trivial some of our biggest problems are once we listen to ourselves explaining them to another!

As a friend of mine used to say when she'd find me feeling sorry for myself, "The good news is that misery is optional."

There are many ways to dedicate ourselves to what lifts us up. I would like to briefly touch on three: Look, listen, and trust.

*Look.* We spend far too much time focused on what's wrong—what needs to be fixed. Why not take time to look for the goodness around us? It is always there, if we are just willing to see it.

This process of looking for the goodness in our lives can lead to what I like to call "gratitude attacks." Relax for a minute. Then think of something you're grateful for: someone dear to you, a specific instance of beauty that has touched you, or the anticipation of an event you are looking forward to. Say, "It is good to be me." More often than not, something else you can be grateful for comes to mind. And then something else—sometimes big, sometimes small—often follows. Savor those good feelings. They are called "bliss," however fleeting they may be.

Let me give you an example from my own experience. With my history of cancer, I often start by being grateful for my health, that I am able to live this one day fully. Before I know it, other thoughts come to mind…my children and the ways they have touched me…my wife and her thoughtfulness…the beauty of colors…the emotions I feel when I hear the song

"I'll Be Home for Christmas"…the fact God *will* come if I let Him. Looking for the goodness around me lifts me up.

*Listen.* Listen to another, to yourself, and to your God. This is harder than it sounds. Listening can be difficult, particularly when we first start, because we aren't used to clearing our mind of all its endless clutter. However, it is well worth the effort because it is a marvelous way to share with another. Listening to our inner longings helps us identify where our bliss may be found. Listening to God—yes, He communicates in all kinds of ways—increases our awareness of His presence within and around us. Listening increases love, and in so doing lifts us up.

*Trust.* Trust that things will work out. Trust that you don't have to do it all. Trust that if you turn your biggest worries over to God, He may handle them at least as well as you have. Trust another, trust yourself, trust your heart. Jesus calls us to be childlike in our trust, because trust dissolves fear and puts color back in our lives. Trust lifts us up.

We are called to the gift of repentance. Let us discard what weighs us down and prepare a way for the Lord so we may be lifted up.

This Advent, spend some time on the gift that is *you.*

*May the waiting god of Advent touch you in your listening heart.*

*May the witness of Mary, the mother of Jesus, inspire you to magnify,*

*to those around you, your own gentleness and beauty of soul.*

*May the Spirit of Jesus be born in you*

*For others to see, a light shining with a radiance of a love that is*

*real, gracious and overflowing.*

—Gregory Norbet

# *Belief*

*Note:* I originally gave this reflection with "Silent Night" playing softly in the background. You may want to do the same when reading and meditating on it. Also, I apologize for the unusual spacing and occasional "Pause" notations. I believe that the material is more meaningful when read at a measured pace and could think of no other way to indicate it.

This is how the birth of Jesus Christ came about.

◆      ◆      ◆

Mary was found with child. In an extraordinary, almost unbelievable way.

She was pregnant, though she had not known man. How could that be?

She had talked to an angel. Come now, who has ever seen an angel?

The angel said, "Be not afraid. God is present.

Mary, you are part of God's plan."

And so, though the circumstances were extraordinary, almost unbelievable, Mary chose to believe.

This is how the birth of Jesus came about.

◆     ◆     ◆

Joseph was confronted with the problem of a pregnant fiancée.

"Some Spirit was involved," she said. Unbelievable!

So God could become one of us,

To be with us in a more personal way.

How could this be?

Then Joseph had a dream.

An angel told him, "Be not afraid. God is present.

You, Joseph, are part of God's plan."

And so, unbelievable as it seemed, Joseph chose to believe.

This willingness to believe in the face of the unbelievable...

this is how the birth of Jesus Christ came about.

◆　　　◆　　　◆

And now, some two thousand years later,

you and I

are Mary and Joseph.

We are asked to believe the unbelievable

So that the birth of Jesus can come about.


In the world at large—

a world torn by hatred, hunger, and hurt—

we are asked to believe

that God is not just the creator of all,

the God of power and might,

but a God who is the everlasting essence

of love, compassion, and gentleness

who desires only our happiness, joy, and fullness of spirit.

Extraordinary. Unbelievable. Yet, we are asked to believe.

Here in our local community,

a world of hurried existences, and whether by choice or necessity,

a world where we each carry a shield of indifference,

we are asked to believe

that our God cries out in sorrow

because we will not acknowledge

His mercy and forgiveness,

Even though they are infinite

and unconditional.

Extraordinary. Almost unbelievable. Yet we are asked to believe.

Finally,

in our own private worlds,

where we live with our fears,

the secrets we dare not share with anyone,

we are asked to believe

that God is truly with us.

That He is responsible for the air we breathe,

the sleep we sleep, the food we eat, the love we love.

We are asked to believe

that this God begs us to give Him our worries,

our concerns, and our heartaches,

so there will be room in our hearts for His Son.

◆      ◆      ◆

This may all seem unbelievable.

But if we dare to believe,

then the birth of Jesus Christ will come about

in the laughs we laugh, the hugs we hug, the songs we sing.

For we, too, are part of God's plan.

Be not afraid.

God is present.

Rejoice in the miracle that is you.

Silent night.

Holy night. All is calm. All is bright.

Christ, our Savior, is born.

# Compassion

Several months ago someone made a puzzling statement to me. He said, "We become what we are."

He didn't just say this to confuse me; he was trying to answer a question I had concerning my mother. She had passed away not long before, within two months of my mother-in-law's death. The dying experience had been very different for the two women. My wife's mother had been accepting, almost eager to get on with it, so to speak, and it was less than two months from the time she had started her final decline until her death. My mother, on the other hand, had lingered for an almost unbelievably long time—almost two years. I was trying to resolve this disparity in my own mind when my acquaintance came up with his explanation: "We become what we are."

When I thought about the two mothers, the statement made sense. Mary (my wife's mother), a delightfully unique person, had always been very accepting of people, points-of-views, and help from others as she aged. My mother, on the other hand, had been more rigid in her approach to life. She was a wonderful woman. Many who knew her would even use the word "classy" to describe her. But she had elected to do more and more for herself during my father's long decline from a series of debilitating illnesses, which ended in his death. In the process, she became fiercely independent. She wanted to be in charge of her life, even to the point of deciding when she was going to die. The behavior patterns, habits, and attitudes formed earlier in both women's lives had become more pronounced in them as they aged. They became more of what they were.

The longer I thought about this statement, the more convinced I became that it applies to all of us—even me. And if it were true (and I was pretty convinced it was), it meant that I could control what I became. This was a really intriguing thought. I began to fantasize about the possibilities.

Then another idea popped into my mind. What would Jesus like me to be?

This provided even more fertile ground for my imagination. Going off to work at a mission in some foreign country had a nice ring to it. (Have you ever noticed that the idea of going somewhere new always sounds like the answer to many questions?) Maybe I should work at simplifying my life—a thought that had occurred to me several times in the past. Maybe I should do more for my family. Thoughts raced through my mind, and then, as if He had spoken, I knew the answer. What would Jesus want me to become? *"Become like me."*

Probably the most consistent and pervasive trait of Jesus' public ministry was his willingness to care. Jesus cared in a radical way. He was drawn to the less fortunate, those treated as failures and outcasts. He loved the unlovable. At the beginning of His ministry, Jesus announced what He perceived his mission to be: to bring glad tidings to the poor, liberty to captives, sight to the blind, and freedom to the oppressed. (Luke 4: 18-19)

Jesus didn't just care; he cared with passion. Jesus performed several healing miracles on the Sabbath, a day to be unsullied by any form of activity by believing Jews (and Jesus was certainly a believing Jew). Every one of these miracles involved someone with long-term problems. Was it really that important if they suffered one more day? And yet, Jesus refused to wait. It was as if He were saying, "I care too much to have these people endure even one more day of their affliction."

When John the Baptist sent disciples to ask Jesus if He was the Messiah, Jesus could have said many things. Yet, what did He say? "Go and tell John what you have seen and heard: the blind regain their sight, the lame walk, lepers are cleansed, the deaf hear, the dead are raised, the poor have the good news proclaimed to them." (Luke 7:22)

Jesus cared with passion about those in need. Jesus was compassionate.

Compassion means to feel what another is feeling. As an old song says, "Walk a mile in my shoes." Compassion involves a willingness to enter into the experience and emotions of another. It is a cornerstone of the structure we call "love." Interestingly, two things almost always happen when we are compassionate. First, we realize that the person is worth caring about, regardless of his or her circumstances. At the same time, we feel an almost irresistible desire to help address what is unacceptable in that person's life.

There is, however, a problem with compassion. We don't like to talk about it, but most of us have an alarm system deep within us which, whenever we encounter someone in need, blares out the warning: "Beware: you have enough problems of your own; you can only handle so much; they created their own problems; don't get entangled." We all do this, and at times we must, if we are to preserve our emotional balance. The trouble is that we tend to make it a habit. While telling ourselves (and others) that we care, we let ourselves believe that what we ignore really doesn't exist. We become imprisoned in a straightjacket of superficiality, unable to fully experience life. Jesus called this habit "hypocrisy."

Fortunately, there is some very good news concerning compassion. Jesus was compassionate because He knew that His Father was compassionate. This means there is no place I can be, no place I can go, where God doesn't feel as I feel and accept me just as I am. What's more, knowing how I feel, God will strive to help. Some refer to this desire as "the divine will to serve."

More good news: we all have the capacity to be compassionate. Think of it as a gift. Saint Paul tells us that we are Christ's body. If Christ's compassion is to be felt in the world, it must be through us. Every one of us has the capacity to bring glad tidings to those impoverished by their loneliness. Through our forgiveness, every one of us can proclaim liberty to people held captive by their mistakes. Every one of us can restore sight to those blinded by the belief that they are unloved. Every one of us can help free those oppressed by fear of rejection. The Spirit of the Lord is with us. Jesus has anointed us. All we need to do is use our gift.

Which brings us to the best news:

As we reach out,
we grow.

In accepting others,
acceptance is ours.

When we forgive,
forgiveness is felt.

Loving
brings the certainty
of being loved.

For compassion given,
is compassion gained.

We become what we are.

# *Humility*

The Beatitudes represent a summary of Jesus' teaching. The fundamental message is one of love—the primacy of love relative to everything else, and in particular, the importance of love for those less fortunate.

Because there was little belief in an afterlife when Jesus lived, the disadvantaged were thought to be receiving their just due for past transgressions. God was thought of primarily as a God of justice. Jesus wanted people to know God as a God of love. Using a very forceful style, Jesus emphasized that God loves the less fortunate; by implication, so should we. His teaching was considered radical in His day. It remains radical today.

As important as this message is, I think that the Beatitudes contain another message, one far more personal in its ramifications for each of us.

Many years ago, almost more than I care to admit, I knew what I wanted: I wanted to be important, to be successful, and to have others look up to me. I thought of it as a race. I would win, and then I would be happy. An aspiring young manager in a large corporation, I soon got the perfect opportunity. I was asked to spend a year working for one of our senior executives. I was delighted, because the senior executive was my hero. For purposes of this story, let's call him George. George was self-assured, knowledgeable, in charge, well respected. He had won the race.

That was what I wanted.

During the next six months, I was surprised to learn how hard George had to work, how much time he spent responding to the demands of others, and how much effort he put into looking prepared. *The price of success*, I thought. Then one evening I received a real shock. Returning to work to pick up some papers, I found George alone in his office, clearly miserable. He looked as if he wanted to cry, but couldn't. The next day I learned the reason why. George had been passed over for the job held by his boss. Despite all his success, despite the sacrifices he had made, he was still running the race, and he thought he was losing.

I wish I could tell you that, based on this valuable lesson, I changed. Sad to say, I did not. Until I had watched the same thing happen over and over; until the person sitting in the office, alone and miserable, wanting to cry but not able to, was me.

I do not tell this story to make you think all business executives have misplaced values. Almost without exception, the ones I met were wonderful people. I tell this story because to some extent, most of us are like George. We want to be happy, yet we think happiness must be earned by doing more.

Over time, I found a better answer in what seemed to be a strange place—the Gospels. They helped me understand *me*. In the Gospels, Jesus talks about attitudes for living. Attitudes for "being" instead of for "doing." As someone once said, "*Be*-attitudes."

The Beatitudes are centered on the gift of humility. That surprised me at first, because like many, I was confused about what humility meant. Somehow I associated it with the idea of humiliation, involving a conscious effort (on my part or someone else's) to degrade me, to make me feel worthless. Humility means something entirely different.

Humility comes from a Latin word, *humus*, which means "earth." Think of humility as being down-to-earth, the willingness to accept others and ourselves as we are, warts and all.

Humility is accepting that we don't have always to be *doing* to be happy. It is knowing that in the final analysis, our happiness depends not so much on what we do or what others think of us. Happiness depends on how we think of ourselves. It is living on the basis that it is good to be me, just the way I am. I prefer to think of it like this: I don't have to be the center of the universe; God already is.

Most of us operate on the premise that we are responsible for life's results, making sure everything turns out for the best. As a consequence, we are forced to pretend that we have our act together, know what we are doing, and have things under control. I don't know if this is because of an expectation level created by others or because of our own insecurities. From my own experience, I do know that it involves endless effort and tends to lock us into a universe that is limited to ourselves.

We don't have to be the center of the universe; God already is. What a relief!

God created us in love. Not one of us is perfect, we make mistakes, we will always have more to do, but it is good to be just who we are…just as we are. What's more, we are never alone; He is always with us, and He wants us to know that when it comes to living, we are responsible only for our own efforts. He will take care of the results in life if we are willing to let him. "Blessed is the one who trusts in the LORD,/whose hope is in the LORD." (Jeremiah 17:7)

All I need to learn is how to be truly me. Jesus said, "Come to me, all you who labor and are burdened, and I will give you rest.…learn from me, for I am meek and humble of heart; and you will find rest for yourselves." (Matthew 11:28-30)

With all this in mind, let me restate Luke's account of the Beatitudes. Perhaps you will find something of value.

Woe is grief, sorrow, and/or emptiness—almost
    always self-imposed.

Woe to you who race after "riches"—things others
    say are important—for the race will be your only
    consolation.
Woe to you who are filled with yourself,
    for you will hunger for love.
Woe to you who laugh to hide the pain inside;
    for you will weep in your loneliness.
Woe to you who try to please everyone so all will
    speak well of you,
    for you will please no one, including yourself.

Blessed is peace-filled happiness, almost always the
    result of one's decisions.

Blessed are you who are poor,
    accepting yourself as you are, others as they are,
    for the kingdom of God—
    the freedom to give and receive love
    unconditionally—
    is yours.
Blessed are you who hunger for enduring
    happiness,
    for you will be satisfied.
Blessed are you who weep,
    you who allow yourself to feel and express
    feelings,

for you will know laughter.

Blessed are you who trust in the Lord,
even when all around you exclude, even insult
you.

Rejoice and be glad, for together there is nothing
you and God cannot do.

# *Hope*

Recently, an acquaintance asked if I would be willing to give a homily about Hope. He remembered being taught at a very early age that there was something special about Faith, Hope, and Love. While there seemed to be much said concerning Faith and Love, he felt there was almost no mention of Hope. Since he also thought he might be missing something, he made his request. After giving it some thought, I realized he was right. I decided I might be missing something, too. This reflection, which I choose to call "Why Settle for Less?" is the result.

Of all living creatures, only humans have the capacity to think about the future. This uniqueness leads to an interesting result. Thinking about the future influences the present. If I have something positive to look forward to, I feel better; if the future looks bleak, I tend to feel the same way. Thinking about the future is not only unique; it is important.

Hope is a one-word description of a way to think about the future. For most of us, hope is *wishing* that something we want to happen will happen, even though we know there's a good chance that it won't. As a die-hard New York Mets fan, I *hope* the Mets will win every game they play. I *hope* the weather will be good tomorrow. I *hope* I will always be in a good mood.

This is not the Hope discussed in the scriptures or the Hope in Faith, Hope, and Love. A far more radical notion, this Hope can be defined as *the willingness to trust in God's goodness.* It means we can live with the certainty that no matter what happens, God will lead us to a better life. No matter how great the pain, things will improve. Obviously, Hope has no meaning in the absence of difficulty. It is when times are darkest that the need for light is most strongly felt.

This radical notion called Hope does not mean that specific events, or even life in general will turn out the *way* we want it to. It also does not that mean life will get better *when* we want it to. The only certainty is that if we are willing to trust, life will get better.

We can apply this idea to specific events or to general life themes. As with so many things, it is our decision. We can be hope-filled or hope-less.

I call this idea of Hope a radical notion, because most of us have a hard time accepting the possibility that it might be true. But wouldn't it be fantastic if we could?

Faith, Hope, and Love are called the "Theological Virtues." That's a fancy way of saying that they are important. Think of them as the cornerstones of a life fully lived. Not just a Christian life, or a spiritual life—even though these are important, but life lived every minute of every day. They are also grouped together because they are related. Just as leaving a key ingredient out of a recipe will produce less than the intended result, so Faith, Hope, and Love can only be fully realized in conjunction with one another. Think of Hope as the chocolate chips in chocolate chip cookies. What would the cookies be like without them? Hope has the same effect on Faith and Love.

Faith is openness to God's love—the willingness to accept that God is present and active in our lives. This is like a light switch. It is either *on* or *off*—either I'm in charge, or God is. "No one can serve two masters." (Matthew 6:24)

Hope gives us reason to be open to God's love. No matter what happens, God will always bring light; things will be all right, no matter what. Jesus was the perfect example. While we don't often think of it this way, Jesus died a failure, but he trusted in God's goodness, and His trust proved more powerful than death. God promises us the same: rebirth to new life after all the deaths in our lives, including the last one.

"Can a mother forget her infant,
    be without tenderness for the child of her womb?
Even should she forget,
    I will never forget you." (Isaiah 49:15).

Hope usually arises from faith. At the same time, hope gives texture, strength, and depth to faith. Think of how bland faith without hope is. Think how much richer a faith with true hope can be. Think of chocolate chips in chocolate chip cookies.

Love involves sharing without condition. Hope frees us to do so.

When I was a very young—maybe six or seven—I saw the movie called *Lassie Come Home.* The plot involves Lassie going through a series of harrowing incidents while trying to get home. I clearly remember my anxiety and worry the first time I saw the movie. Would Lassie make it home safely? I was a wreck by the end of the movie.

About three weeks later, for reasons I can't remember, I saw the movie for a second time. The movie was the same, but my reaction was completely different. I was relaxed. I noticed the other characters in the movie. I even laughed a couple of times. The *only* difference was that I knew how the movie ended. I knew everything would turn out all right. This is the promise of Hope. Knowing that everything will turn out all right allows us to worry less and relax more.

Just imagine the emotional energy we waste each day worrying, trying to make things turn out the way we want them to. And how successful are we? Lord knows there are enough problems each day without our adding to them! Jesus calls us to Hope when He says, "Do not worry about your life." (Matthew 6:25) Free yourself to focus your energies on what you can affect today: the love you give, the love you receive, the ability to share without condition.

Hope frees us to love more fully. Loving more fully helps things turn out for the best, which brings us to the subtle yet miraculous quality of true Hope. It tends to be self-fulfilling. Check it out for yourself.

Faith with Hope brings serenity. Love with Hope brings joy. They are the cornerstones of a life fully lived, because they are the cornerstones of the kingdom.

So don't worry about your life. Hope for the best!

Why settle for less?

# *Sin*

Freedom is a cherished value in our society. We have fought wars in its name, have written laws to protect it, and we live in a society that constantly reinforces the importance of being "free to be all you can be." The question is this: Does God want us to be free?

We are taught that God has given us free will, but it seems that He has also given us plenty of rules to follow: Ten Commandments, eight Beatitudes, and countless dos and don'ts from our church leaders. As a child, I fretted over how many things I was supposed to remember, and I worried that I might forget something important. When you add the notion that Jesus will be coming back to judge how well we have done—sort of a great policeman in the sky—you can really begin to wonder, does God want us to be free?

The story of Jesus and the adulterous woman in John's Gospel helps answer this question. This story deals with the subject of freedom, because it deals with the subject of sin. The two are connected.

We don't talk about sin much any more. It's almost as if it has gone out of style. We pay lip service to the wrongness of sin, but seldom think about it. Sin seems to be increasingly associated (in our minds, if nowhere else) with fun—free use of God's gifts to gratify our senses so we may live more fully. In the movie *Usual Suspects,* the anti-hero makes a profound point when he claims that Satan's greatest accomplishment is convincing our generation that he no longer exists.

Sin obviously does still exist, but it is not as glamorous as it may seem. Sin can be defined as any abuse of God's gifts that leads to separation in our relationships—separation from others, from God, and, most especially, from ourselves.

Relationships are critical to knowing who we are and how we are doing. They form the mirror we use to see ourselves. Separation from relationships always reduces our freedom because this separation involves a diminishment of self—a reduction in our sense of self-worth and our ability to successfully deal with life.

Consider the adulteress when Jesus encounters her in John's Gospel. There she is, in front of a crowd, her wrongdoing made public. Imagine her embarrassment. If you have a hard time experiencing this feeling, think of something you've done wrong in your past—that secret you don't want anyone to know. We all have them. Then imagine standing in front of all your acquaintances while your secret is revealed. The resulting embarrassment is caused by guilt, shame, remorse, or some combination of all three. Think of these emotions as prison bars, for they all lead to fear, and fear is the cornerstone of the prison of separation.

I think there are two particularly insidious things about sin. The first relates to our nature. By nature we are good, and our instinct is to do the right thing. As a result, almost all sin starts out with someone thinking he or she is taking an action that will produce some good. We call this "temptation." Ask the addict dying from substance abuse why he wants more, and he will tell you he only wants to feel better. We tend to have good intentions, but struggle with denial when the result is bad. We even create rationalizations for evil, usually some form of "the end justifies the means."

The second insidious thing about sin is its progressive nature when unrecognized and unacknowledged. Little sins tend to lead to larger ones. The result is a vicious circle. A small mistake creates a feeling of regret. A slightly larger misstep, usually directed at regaining a sense of emotional balance, leads to a greater sense of alienation, and so on. Once again, substance abuse provides an excellent example; increasing the consumption of alcohol, drugs, or pills to compensate for increasing anxiety when sober leads to increased emotional isolation. Evil, when allowed to grow, always results in separation from free will.

Sin is serious business. Complete separation from all relationships, the pain of complete isolation from love, is hell. I'm not sure what it's like in the next life, but I've met people already there in this one. Perhaps you have, too.

What is God's role in all this?

To begin with, He gave us free will. Free will means there must be good and bad, virtue and sin. If not, the gift of free will would be an empty gesture. Does God get upset with our inevitable mistakes? Did God send Jesus to judge our wrong-doings? How does God act toward sinners? The following Gospel passages help answer all three questions.

"He...said to them, 'Let the one among you who is without sin be the first to throw a stone at her.'" (John 8:7-8)

God created us. He knows we are all sinners. He understands and loves us unconditionally, just as we are. This is a very simple idea, but one we find very difficult to believe. Sometimes I wonder what our world would be like if we would only accept ourselves the way God accepts us.

"Then Jesus said, 'Neither do I condemn you.'" (John 8:11)

We often forget it, but Jesus never judged anyone. He was critical of patterns of behavior, but His call to judgment was and still is an invitation to judge ourselves so we can rid ourselves of all that prevents us from being free. Over and over again in the Gospels, Jesus focuses on His Father's forgiveness. He knows that unconditional love means unconditional forgiveness. The problem isn't God; the problem is our unwillingness to accept forgiveness. It takes courage to face past mistakes, to share them with another, or to let go of the emotional waste associated with them. But it is our choice, not God's.

"Then Jesus said to her, 'Woman, where are they?…go, and from now on do not sin any more.'" (John 8:10-11)

God is not only willing to forgive, He is willing to forget. His reaction to our mistakes is to help disperse the crowd, removing the reasons for shame, guilt, even despair. God encourages us to let go of the past and allow ourselves to start anew.

God calls us, sinners all, to freedom. He has even provided ground rules for healthy relationships; we call them the Ten Commandments and eight Beatitudes. Think of them as a road map to healthy relationships. God *commands* us to live full and free lives. For those who might have difficulty remembering them all, Jesus even simplified the whole idea: love one another as I have loved you.

God loves us just as we are. He is always ready to forgive. He calls us to let go of what is past and start anew on our journey so we can be free to be all we can be.

# Spring

# *Forgiveness*

The tale of the prodigal son may be the best known of all Jesus' parables. In telling the story, Jesus was responding to some law-abiding citizens who had questioned his continued preoccupation with those they considered unworthy. The main character is an obvious sinner who is given a feast, while his righteous older brother refuses to join the party.

The story did not appear to affect Jesus' critics, but they have been the exceptions. For two thousand years this story has touched people. The baffling graciousness of the father, the younger son's unmerited good fortune, the apparent discrimination against the older son, and even the inconclusive ending all have something to do with our continued fascination. The most important reason for the popularity of this parable is that it deals with the mystery of forgiveness.

The story quickly establishes that the younger son is an unsavory character. Rudeness toward his father, turning his back on all he should value, and squandering his fortune in immoral ways are obvious shortcomings. What is not so apparent to us now, is that a Jewish son of that time, particularly a second son, would never dream of asking for his inheritance. In doing so, he is committing a form of murder, for in effect, he is declaring his father dead. Even his motivation for returning to his father is completely self-centered. He is hungry.

And yet when he returns home, he is forgiven.

We Christians spend an inordinate amount of time worrying about and praying for God's forgiveness. This is sad, because Jesus was very clear in declaring that God always forgives. That is what God does. Jesus went so far as to say that the only sin that cannot be forgiven is an unwillingness to accept forgiveness. (1)

Scripture tells us that God not only forgives—He forgets. When the prodigal son returns, the father has been eagerly waiting for him, unconcerned with the son's past mistakes, current motivation, or carefully crafted apology. He is consumed with joy and concerned only with a lavish display of his affection. Unconditional love includes unconditional forgiveness.

If this is true, why do we continue to fret about God's forgiveness? Are we the problem? The story of the prodigal son helps answer this question in its portrayal of the choices made by the two brothers.

The younger son initially chooses to separate himself from all that is important. By doing it *his way*, he ends up in the worst possible circumstances: penniless, hungry, and feeding animals that represent all that is unclean. Realizing the error of his ways, he makes a second choice. He returns home, accepts his father's forgiveness, and begins a new life with a celebratory feast.

Then there is the older brother. Based on our initial impression, we tend to identify with him—trying to do the right thing in the face of unfair treatment by others—but his choices place him in this position. His pride and anger separate him from his father. His eagerness to judge and unwillingness to forgive separate him from his younger brother. Will he change his mind and choose to join the celebration, thereby experiencing new life? The story ends with that question unanswered. But it prompts another question: How often are we the older brother?

God always forgives. The question is whether or not we are willing to accept his forgiveness. Recognizing the wrongs we have done, acknowledging our faults, and expressing regret for them are important steps in accepting forgiveness, but the key is our willingness to forgive ourselves. We forgive ourselves by forgiving others. The whole idea is summarized in the Lord's Prayer: "Forgive us...as we forgive others." Notice the key word is "as," not "because."

We do not earn forgiveness. It is a gift we accept every time we decide to forgive. There is no magic in this process. It is simply the way we are. Jesus makes this whole idea very clear when Peter asks him how often he must forgive. Jesus answers, "I say to you not seven times, but seventy-seven times." (Matthew 18:22) The number seven connotes infinity.

We must always forgive. Jesus goes on to explain why by using the parable of the unforgiving debtor. Moved with compassion, a king forgives a huge debt. The one forgiven refuses to forgive a much smaller debt (does this sound like the older brother?), and as a result, the king withdraws his forgiveness. "If you forgive men their transgressions, your heavenly Father will forgive you. But if you do not forgive men, neither will your Father forgive your transgressions." (Matthew 6:14) We accept forgiveness by forgiving others.

Forgiveness is a choice, not a feeling. When we forgive, we are refusing to be burdened with mistakes made by others. We are refusing to let others determine our happiness. We are refusing to separate ourselves from life.

Harboring resentment against another is like taking poison and waiting for the other person to die. It dampens, and then destroys our ability to celebrate life. Forgiving another is forgiving ourselves, freeing us from guilt about the past and anxieties concerning the future.

Shortly before his death from cancer, Bishop Leo O'Neill of Manchester, New Hampshire, spoke at what he knew would be his last public appearance. He said his only wish was that we would all be willing to forgive. In his final days he had gained a deepened appreciation for the priceless nature of each day we live. Why waste the smallest part of even one single day carrying the burden of unnecessary emotional baggage?

The story of the prodigal son is about the choices we make in the face of God's goodness. This story might be more aptly named "the story of the forgiving father." Jesus is telling us that it is God's nature to eagerly await our return whenever we separate ourselves from Him. When we make the decision to return, regardless of our reasoning, God rushes to us, showering us with His forgiveness, leading us to new life. When we are self-centered in the choices we make, He even pleads with us, "Everything I have is yours." (Luke 15: 31)

God's goodness is complete and transforming. God calls us to celebrate life. Forgiveness is our God-given way to join the celebration, both now and forever.

1. Hans Küng, *On Being a Christian*, p. 210

# *Suffering*

We seldom discuss suffering in church. It's almost as if coming to church provides an invisible shield to protect us from harm. Yet isn't it interesting that the longest Gospel passage of the year, the account of Jesus' crucifixion, is centered on suffering? Suffering is part of life, even a Christian life well lived.

All of us have known suffering in one form or another. While individual experiences vary, they all have at least one thing in common. When we suffer, we are not just aware of our discomfort; we tend to become consumed by it. Suffering centers our attention on self. Almost invariably, we wonder why we must experience this pain. We look for a reason. Explanations abound, but all too often we feel the way Job must have felt when God answered his question about suffering by saying, in effect, "Who are you to question?" Suffering just is a part of God's creation.

Suffering is one of the most important mysteries in life. It can distort, even destroy, our well-being. At the same time, it can be the birthplace of exceptional personal growth. Since there is no simple explanation for its existence, we tend to assign responsibility to the Divine. If God is a God of love, why is

His creation filled with suffering? If God knows me and is with me, is He responsible for my suffering? When I am in pain; is God punishing me?

At least on the surface, Jesus doesn't seem to help. He never made an effort to explain suffering. The key prayer He taught his disciples—the Our Father—contains seven petitions. Not one mentions suffering. In fact, Jesus seemed to embrace pain. "Whoever wishes to come after me must deny himself, take up his cross, and follow me." (Matthew 16:24) I do not find this particularly appealing advice, particularly after reading an account of Jesus' crucifixion.

At the risk of oversimplifying, it seems to me there are two kinds of suffering. The first kind involves what we can understand, while the second deals with suffering that is beyond our understanding.

Most positive change involves some level of discomfort, or *understandable* suffering. Self-help books abound with advice that amounts to the truism, "no pain, no gain." If you don't think so, just ask any mother how childbirth felt. Another kind of understandable suffering involves that which is self-induced. I am talking here about suffering caused by bad habits, reckless behavior, treatable illnesses like alcoholism, or damaging attitudes triggered by low self-esteem. Since we are responsible for the pain, we control when it stops. Suffering serves a useful purpose, because it can provide an incentive to change.

Finally, understandable suffering can result from deciding to do the right thing, even when it is not the easy thing: telling the truth when the truth hurts, defending an unpopular acquaintance, helping those in need when doing so involves sharing their pain. I don't think Jesus died on the cross because it was God's will that He do so. Jesus was crucified because He refused to stop doing what He knew was right. In this sense, He was obedient to the will of His Father—obedient to the point of death.

While understandable suffering is not so mysterious, some suffering defies explanation. It is random, almost capricious, causing great anguish for no discernible reason: a sudden death; a life-threatening illness; starving children in our world, country, or town; the harm we inflict, whether by suicide bombings or domestic abuse. We feel like screaming, "My God, why have you abandoned us? How can you let this happen?" One personal story will help make my point.

A young woman—let's call her Gina for the sake of this story—did everything right. She had a healthy upbringing—loving her family, doing well in school, and attending church regularly. She was attractive and a joy to be around. During college she met a nice young man, and after college, they decided to get married. Everything was perfect—until their wedding night, when he started to beat her. What followed was twelve months of hell for Gina. The degradation caused by physical suffering was almost less important than the emotional pain. (How can this be? What I have done to cause this? Isn't there any way to fix him?) Finally, after extensive but fruitless counseling, Gina was forced to seek a divorce.

Some suffering defies understanding.

Which brings us back to the question, what is God's involvement in suffering? I would like to offer a three-part answer. While it is based on personal experience, I believe scripture supports the answer, particularly in what Jesus said and did.

First, God is responsible for suffering in the sense that it is clearly part of His creation. However, I do not believe that God overtly causes individual suffering. It is part of life. The issue is not why we are given what life hands us, but how we will deal with what we receive.

The second thing we can say about God's involvement in suffering is that there is no suffering we can experience that He, in the form of Jesus, has not already experienced. There is no place suffering can take us where we will not find Him. The obvious mistake we all make when reading a Gospel account of Jesus' passion is that we do so knowing what will happen next. Try reading it while pretending it is the last chapter.

The first time I did this, I was reduced to tears. Jesus suffered physically: the whipping, the thorns in his head, the exhaustion from no rest, the pain of carrying the cross, the nails in hands and feet, the act of slowly suffocating to death once the cross was raised. He suffered mentally: betrayed by a comrade, denied by his friends, stripped of everything—even his clothing—and dying a death so degrading it was reserved for only the most despicable criminals. He suffered emotionally: rejected by all but a few, so desperately lonely that He prayed, "My God, my God, why have you forsaken me?" (Matthew 27:46) The Divine feels our suffering. God suffers when we do. This is one of the reasons so many find God viscerally present in the midst of their suffering.

Finally, I believe God will always bring good from suffering when He is allowed to do so. I leave it to you to decide whether this is because of overt action on His part or simply the way His creation works. In either case, it is God's nature to bring goodness. It is also his nature to allow us—you could even say require us—to participate in the process.

I doubt if anyone would argue that suffering changes us. The only question is "how?" Some grow, becoming more capable of dealing with the challenges of life. A common metaphor in the Jewish scriptures compares suffering to the process of shaping fine metals in the heat of a furnace. Unfortunately, others seem to retreat, trying to insulate themselves from pain while they wait for life to treat them more kindly.

The prominent psychiatrist Dr. Viktor Frankl was the author of *Man's Search for Meaning*, which recounts his experiences in a Nazi concentration camp. Everyone there lost everything, including family and possessions—even, in most cases, the will to live. Why, then, did some not just survive, but actually grow in depth and awareness? Why did increases in suffering seem to foster increased personal growth for a few?

In the end, Dr. Frankl concluded that suffering centers us on self to the point where we are forced to realize that the only real freedom we have is an inner freedom—the ability to choose our attitudes. The ones who choose to find meaning in their life—whether it be in the form of loved ones, hope for the future, or trust in the Divine—are the ones who not only survive, but grow in depth and compassion. Isn't it interesting that one of the most common by-products of suffering is increased compassion, which leads to an increased ability to comfort, or even heal, others?

We say, "My God, my God, why have you forsaken me?" (Matthew 27:46) God says, "My children, my children, why have you forsaken me?"

Job learned that he would never understand why suffering existed. He learned that his friends weren't always helpful. The most important thing he learned, however, was to trust, trust, even when understanding fails. God did not forsake Job. Gina may never know why she went through the pain of her first marriage, but somehow she knew to trust, even when understanding failed. Today she is happily remarried, the mother of a beautiful young son, more aware than you or I of what goodness means. Her lights are brighter because more than you or I, she has experienced the dark.

We may never understand our suffering, but we can live with
the certainty that when we trust, carrying our pain rather than
being buried by it, God will not forsake us.

Suffering happens.
Sometimes annoying,
sometimes searing,
always centering.

Jesus said,
"Trust in me.
Deny yourself.
Take up your cross,
follow me."

"Through suffering
to the resurrection.
Trust in me."

# *Resurrection*

It is hard to overstate the importance of Jesus' resurrection. Without this pivotal event, it is almost certain that only those who knew Him most intimately would have remembered Jesus, although even those people probably would have thought of Him as a well-intended failure.

This is why all four Gospel accounts present the resurrection in such detail. The tomb, a symbol of death and defeat, is empty. An angel, a sign of God's involvement, is present to announce the good news. Women are the first to hear of this miraculous occurrence, signifying the vital importance of women to the survival of early Christianity. And finally, in Matthew's account both the angel and Jesus say, "Be not afraid." Resurrections should be a cause for joy, rather than fear of the previously unknown.

It is clear from Jesus' ministry that He believed in life after death. It is also clear that most people He encountered could not or would not accept this reality. In the intervening centuries, it appears that very little has changed.

During the last half of the twentieth century, a woman named Elisabeth Kübler-Ross started writing and speaking out about death and dying. She was attempting to reduce the stigma associated with death. In her own way, she was saying, "Be not afraid."

One of the most interesting aspects of her research was the consistency of what became known as near-death experiences: brief periods of time when someone came close to, or actually died physically before regaining consciousness. Feelings of light, warmth, and a great peace were almost universally experienced.

Most of us would still prefer to avoid the subjects of death and resurrection. This is partially caused by our fear of the unknown, but perhaps this tendency is also caused by our conviction that death—and resurrection to the extent that we believe in it—happen only once, at the end of things. Nothing could be further from the truth.

"Death" can be defined as leaving life as we know it—an ending. "Resurrection" refers to starting a new life that holds the potential to be better than the existence we left behind. Think of this process as a difficult, but meaningful transition.

The unique aspect of this change is that we have a choice in the matter. While we cannot avoid leaving the life that was, we do get to decide whether or not we are willing to make the transition to a new and more complete life. In effect, we are asked the question, "Do you choose life?"

Life can be viewed as a cycle of deaths and potential resurrections; this is often difficult, but always meaningful. Dying and rising again is what life is all about.

Sometime around twenty-four months old, a child starts asserting his or her independence. This time is often referred to as the "terrible twos," because it clearly involves a difficult, but meaningful, transition. Around twelve years old, this same child will start rebelling against parental authority based on a need for even greater independence. We call this "adolescence." Once again, it can be a difficult time for all involved. Finally, in the early twenties, as the child matures, parents suddenly recover their wisdom and become more desirable company. While less stressful for parents, this can be a difficult time for the young adult as he or she adjusts to living the life of a mature adult.

In all three cases, the individual involved leaves life as he or she knows it and begins an existence that, although it includes much of the old, is focused on a new way of living. The decision to move from one stage of life to another becomes a more conscious one as we get older. Those unable or unwilling to make these transitions are considered "abnormal." In this life, "growing up" is the norm.

Death and resurrection events are not limited to the aging process. Life is filled with them: marriage, having children, serious illness, and the loss of a loved one through death or divorce, to name a few. In every case, one must decide whether to leave the life that was and begin life anew, with the potential for the new life to be better than the old. Let me share a true story that illustrates this point.

Almost nine years ago a young woman in her mid-twenties left her apartment for work around six-thirty in the morning. She and her husband lived in a major metropolitan area, and she had to walk approximately fifty yards to a detached garage. She noticed a man leaning against a telephone pole, watching her. He made her nervous, so she started to walk faster. He began to move toward her. She ran to her car, hoping to enter it before he could reach her. He was too quick, grabbing her and ripping the car keys from her hand. He opened the trunk, threw her in, and then drove the car from the garage. Over the next fourteen hours, he repeatedly abused the young woman, finally dumping her in an alley, presumably to die. Fortunately, she was discovered by a local policeman and rushed to a nearby hospital. When her sister arrived at the hospital, she rushed into the emergency room but walked past the young woman. The physical bruising was so great that she was unrecognizable.

This young woman was one of our daughters. While she had been born to a different family, we had helped raise her, and had always referred to her and her sister as our heart-adopted daughters. When I first learned what had happened, I felt paralyzed. I could not make my body move. I think I was in shock. I finally called her later that night, and before I could say anything she said something I will never forget: "Don't worry, Bill; there is nothing God and I can't handle."

In many ways, this young woman literally died that terrible day. Over a span of years, she has had to relearn many of the ordinary things of life. She and her husband (most marriages fail to survive this kind of tragedy) have had to work closely and relentlessly with trained therapists. It has not been easy, and it has often hurt, but this young woman made a decision—a decision to live. Today, she still carries scars from her experience, but she is also more alive—more vibrant, caring, thoughtful, and decisive—than before her tragedy. She and her husband have a stronger marriage. They also have a beautiful young daughter.

Resurrections happen.
God is involved
in every resurrection.

No matter what the death,
He will bring life, new light,
new horizons,
when we decide to live.

Then the final resurrection
And one last decision:
Do you chose life?

We stand with the scars of life,
in light, warmth, and peace.
The angel whispers,
"Be not afraid."

We are home,
at peace
in God.
No more deaths—
Forever.

# *Love*

What is love? For a long time I pondered this question.

We all know that love is important. Almost instinctively, we sense that we can't live without it. Yet, what is *it*?

We are told there are many kinds of love. Our music, our literature, even our conversations are filled with references to it. The evangelist John says we cannot know God without loving, for God is love. Jesus, when leaving His apostles, tells them that the most important thing to remember is to "love one another." (John 15:17) He makes it his *one* commandment. Jesus even says that He is telling them this so their joy might be complete. Love sounds wonderful. But what is love?

For most of us, the mention of love conjures up images of romantic love—the emotional and sexual attraction that comes from strong feelings for another. Yet romantic love is but one form of love. The Easter season teaches us that love is powerful—more powerful than death. Love promises resurrection, new life. And scripture defines love in various ways. Paul, in perhaps the best-known dissertation on love, tells the

Corinthians that love is patient. Love is also kind. Love is never jealous. Love delights in the truth. Love never ends.

Love seems to be many things.

When I ask what love is, I receive various answers:
"Love is being nice to people."
Not enough, I think.
"Love is…well, you know, love is love."
I don't think this gets me very far.
And then the best one:
"Your question cannot be answered, for love is a mystery."
Love may be a mystery, but if I want to love another as Jesus commanded, what am I supposed to do? How do I know I am getting it right? When all is said and done, *what is love?*

Love does have countless dimensions and truly is a mystery, but I have come to believe that all forms of love have, at their core, a common ingredient. Love always involves *a willingness to share, without condition.* That sharing may come in the form of giving away: I give you a hug, a smile, my clothing, my time. Sharing may also be in the form of giving up, of letting go: a resentment, a feeling, the desire to control.

Sharing is not the stuff of love unless it involves sharing without condition, giving away or giving up, with no strings attached.

Remember when you were young and a parent or baby sitter would say to you, "I will read you this story if you are good" or "I will give you a cookie if you behave"? Perhaps you have done the same with your own children. The problem for most of us is that we never outgrow this idea of conditional behavior. It becomes ingrained in our approach to life. I will share what I am feeling if you act the way I think you should act. I will give you what you want if you say "please." I will love you when you are nice to me.

Conditional sharing is not love, even when great kindness is involved. Love always involves a willingness to share without condition.

How do I know this? Jesus' command was to "love one another as I love you." (John 15:12) I don't really know why, but for a long time I thought this meant "Love one another *because* I love you," but one day I realized that Jesus was saying, "Love one another *the way* I have loved you. *Do* what I have done." *This is easy,* I thought to myself. If I want to know what love is, all I have to do to study what Jesus did most often. And when I did, it dawned on me that Jesus was *always* willing to share, without condition.

Jesus did many things during his public ministry. But the thing He did most often, the most common trait, was this: He communicated. He taught, told stories, explained His actions, asked if His listeners understood Him, and prayed. No one ever had any trouble knowing how He felt, what His opinions were. Jesus knew the importance of being willing to share His thoughts and His feelings, without condition.

Love is communicating: sharing our thoughts and our feelings. Fifty percent of all marriages end in divorce, and the most common reason for divorce is a lack of meaningful communication. "I'm not sure what happened; we just stopped talking about anything important. We became strangers." Our relationships determine how we feel about ourselves; they define how we view life. They are the strongest influence on our ability to grow as human beings, and the lifeblood of healthy relationships is good communication.

Love is the willingness to work at communicating—communicating without condition. When we do, when I am willing to tell you how I am *really* feeling, rather than the normal "Hi, How are you?" "I'm fine, how are you?" "I'm fine too, isn't the weather nice?" it is a tremendously freeing experience. It is a way to relieve tension, dispel fear, and encourage intimacy. It is the currency of joyful living.

One of the things Jesus talked about most often was forgiveness. His sayings and parables are filled with references to the subject. He seemed to be saying, "Forgive as your Father forgives." Forgive unconditionally, which is exactly what Jesus did. "Father, forgive them; they know not what they do." (Luke 23:34) Forgiveness is important. It frees us from destructive resentments. It clears blockages in relationships. Forgiveness sets us free.

Jesus' most frequent activity in the gospels involved His efforts to heal. Jesus had a gift for healing. He was willing to share that gift, without condition. In almost every healing miracle, Jesus showed that He cared, was willing to reach out and try to heal, even at risk to Himself, *and* never asked for anything in return. He never attached conditions.

We all have gifts. We are all healers when we are willing to share our gifts: to risk caring, to reach out and touch others, *and* to do so without condition. The interesting thing is that we feel better when we do so. The gifts we share seem to grow, to become more. We experience life more fully. We experience a sense of joy.

Finally, Jesus was willing to share the unsharable. Once again, He did so without condition. If you aren't sure what I mean, take a close look at a crucifix next time you're in church. "No one has greater love than this, to lay down one's life for one's friends." (John 15:13)

Very few of us have been, or will ever be faced with the prospect of giving up our life for another. But almost all of us have been in relationships where we have had the opportunity to do something that seemed on the surface impossible to do. It's called sharing the unsharable: accepting someone just the way he or she is, letting a loved one make his or her own mistakes, forgiving when forgiveness is impossible, looking someone straight in the eye and saying—yes, you've got it—"I love you."

Love is many things, but love always involves a willingness to share unconditionally. God is love, because God always shares unconditionally. God shows no partiality. The great truth of life is that when we share in the same way we become more. We bear fruit. We experience the joy of knowing love.

> This is my commandment:
> love one another
> as I love you.
> I have told you this
> so my joy may be in you
> and your joy may be complete.
>
> —John 15:12, 11

# *Trinity*

On Trinity Sunday we celebrate the nature of our God: three persons in one God. This is one of the most important doctrines in our Christian faith tradition. For the longest time, however, the thought of celebrating the Trinity bothered me. Like most Christians, I had been taught that the Trinity was a mystery, something we could never understand. How do you celebrate something you can't understand? It seemed to me to be roughly analogous to holding a party for a stranger.

What helped dispel this confusion was the realization that I do not have to understand something to know it. Let me use two examples to explain. A great number of us use cell phones. Do you understand how they work? I don't, but I *know* they do, so they are part of my life. How many people understand how airplanes stay in the air? I don't, but I can promise you I am very glad they do every time I am at twenty-five thousand feet looking out the window at those seemingly flimsy wings. I am willing to risk my life on something I don't understand because I *know* airplanes really do fly.

A mystery is something we know exists because we have experienced it, even though we can't explain it.

Human nature involves many mysteries. Why are some people willing to expose themselves to extreme, sometimes life-threatening danger in the name of doing what's right? Why are some people unwilling to deal with the fears that keep them from leading healthy lives while others find it so easy to enter into intimate relationships that allow them to blossom?

I used to think I knew the answer to these questions, and many others like them, but the longer I am involved in listening to people who need someone to talk to, the less sure I am. All I know is that these conditions exist. As a teacher I admire once said, "The more I know, the less I understand."

One of life's greatest mysteries is love. Love involves sharing with another person. But when we give and give of ourselves, don't we run out at some point? Don't we lose ourselves? Does the phrase "the two shall become one" mean I am no longer me? These are reasonable questions for someone who has never known love.

Anyone who has been in a loving relationship knows from experience that as we give, we receive. We become more, not less. We grow as individuals as we become more intimate with another, yet knowing a loved one does mean we understand him or her. My father, shortly after my mother had done something surprising on their fiftieth wedding anniversary, looked at me with a smile and said, "I'm almost sure I know her better than anyone on earth, but I don't think I will ever understand her."

A mystery is something we do not understand, but we still know it because it is part of our lived experience. Knowing the Trinity as part of our lived experience is not just possible, but important, because recognizing the presence of the Divine in our life increases our sense of well-being. Unfortunately, confusion surrounding the Trinity makes it unnecessarily difficult for most of us to experience the reality of the Trinity in our daily lives. I would like to suggest a simple way to deal with this confusion.

As Christians, we refer to three "persons" in one God. Using names like Father, Son, Spirit, even Mother, helps us understand what God is like, because these names evoke images we are familiar with. This is why Jesus, as well as others in scriptures, used them. The problem arises when we carry these images too far and try to imagine three people as one God. The original understanding of the word "person" was not intended to refer to human beings. It meant three distinct, pervasive characteristics. God is not a set of super human beings, joined in some inexplicable way. God is not human. God is love. The Trinity is a reflection of three distinct aspects or characteristics of one love.

God the Father is the creator and the great provider. There is no life without God the Father. All love seeks to create and provide for the one who is loved. God the Father is the pervasive, yet distinct power of love to create and sustain. When we experience ongoing creation, we encounter God, the source of and power behind all creation.

God the Son reveals his Father's love. John even referred to Jesus as the "Word" of God. All love wants to be known. Think of your own experience with someone you love. You want that person to know more about you, just as you want to know more about that person. You want to share yourself, recognizing that sharing leads to greater intimacy, which in turn leads to a more loving approach to life in general. When we witness how the sharing of love changes the way people think and act, we are witnessing the power of God. This is what Jesus was and still is telling us.

God the Spirit helps us change by providing comfort, healing, and counsel. All love seeks to comfort and heal the hurts of the one loved. All love tries to help the one who is loved deal with the inevitable challenges of life. Whenever we experience comfort, or a healing gesture, or a word of well-meant advice that turns out to be almost miraculously helpful, we experience the gentle touch of God's Spirit, regardless of how we receive the comfort, healing, or advice. For the Spirit of God is pervasive and intimately present in our lives.

The Trinity represents
pervasive yet distinct
forces of love
in our lived experience.

God calls us to Trinity.

To create
a new idea, a new friend, a new world.
For as we create,
we become more.

To share,
revealing who and what we are,
For as we share, we save.
As we save, we are saved.

To let our spirits sing
when we comfort and heal,
For as we comfort, we are comforted.
As we heal, we are healed.

God calls us to Trinity.
Now
And forever,
For the Trinity is our destiny—
Love brought to completion.

# Summer

# *Priorities*

Several years ago I gave a homily about "Priorities," based on some of Jesus' sayings in Chapter 10 of Matthew's Gospel. Immediately afterward, a friend of mine stopped to talk to me as people were leaving church. He questioned whether I was portraying Jesus correctly in my preaching. I can't remember what my response was at the time, but I do remember that in the days that followed, I decided that my friend was right in at least one way. I had become too concerned with making Jesus likable.

I thought back to my reaction the first time I had read the Gospels in their entirety. I had been struck by the feeling that quite often Jesus wasn't the slightest bit concerned with being likable. In fact, He seemed to go out of His way to make people feel uncomfortable.

Of course I promptly forgot about what I have just recounted until recently when once again I was given the opportunity to reflect on the same sayings from Matthew. I hope the following more accurately reflects the biblical Jesus.

In His actions and words, Jesus demonstrated that He clearly understood His priorities. There were just three: the importance of God, a bias toward those considered unworthy, and the command to love.

Jesus' first and most consuming priority concerned the importance of God. God was the only absolute—the unchanging source of all goodness. Everything else was less important: money, possessions, what you wore, your job, what group you belonged to, who ran the government, even your family. In Matthew's Gospel Jesus says, "Whoever loves father or mother…son or daughter more than me is not worthy of me." (Matthew 10:37) In Luke's Gospel, Jesus is even more definite. "If anyone comes to me without hating his father and mother, wife and children, brothers and sisters, and even his own life, he cannot be my disciple." (Luke 14:26-27) Yes, for Jesus, everything else was less important.

Jesus knew that we all have some absolute in our lives—something more important than anything else. For the vast majority of us, this absolute is ourselves. Jesus called it being self-righteous; today we would call it self-will or being self-centered.

When I use these words, I am not referring to a healthy self-esteem. I am talking about wanting to be in control, to fix others, to be part of the "in" group, to be better than others, to know we are good or right while others are bad or wrong.

Jesus asked His potential followers a simple question: "Who's in charge, you or God?" He was adamant that there was no third alternative. "No one can serve two masters; He will either hate one and love the other, or be devoted to one and despise the other." (Matthew 6:24)

Jesus went so far as to define the opposite of faith not as doubt, but anxiety, worry and needless fear—those feelings that prevent us from opening ourselves to the power of God's touch. He was certain that only in God could true happiness be found. Our challenge lay in accepting this reality. "Let go," Jesus seemed to be saying. "Let go of everything," meaning let go of your worries and fears concerning everything, even your life. "Whoever finds his life will lose it, and whoever loses his life for my sake will find it." (Matthew 10:39)

Not easy, is it? No wonder His apostles had a hard time accepting Jesus' teachings. No wonder Jesus had to say, "Do you not yet understand or comprehend? Are your hearts hardened?" (Mark 8:17-18)

Jesus' two other priorities were related to his first. One involved His overwhelming bias for those considered unworthy. He spent the preponderance of His time with or talking about those excluded because of their imperfections: sinners, outcasts, and individuals disadvantaged by disease or society. He used those hated by "good" people as role models: tax collectors, the Good Samaritan, a Roman centurion.

It seemed that every time Jesus had a meal, He was eating with the excluded, criticizing those who were doing the excluding, or inviting in someone who wasn't suppose to be there. His first Beatitude asserted that happiness could be found in poverty—a condition every good person sought to avoid. He even told His followers that He would always be found in the midst of those most shunned: the least of their brothers and sisters.

When someone referred to Him as "Good Master," Jesus responded in an interesting way. "Why do you call me good? No one is good but God alone." (Luke 18:19) "His sun rises on the bad and the good, and causes rain to fall on the just and the unjust." (Matthew 5:45) Jesus asserted that those who thought of themselves as "good" were being hypocritical. The "good" tended to assume that strict adherence to rules would earn them God's love. Jesus knew that His father loved each of us unconditionally. The "good" operated on the premise that anyone unlike them was "bad." Jesus knew we all have good and bad within us. The "good" lived on the basis that they did not need to change. Jesus knew that we all need to change. In fact, Jesus asserted that happiness could be found in poverty of spirit, accepting the fact that we need help to change. Jesus went out of His way to include those excluded by others because He also knew that those who recognized their need would be more willing to accept help.

How to receive help? His response was as clear as it was discomforting. "Whoever does not take up his cross and follow after me is not worthy of me." (Matthew 10:38) This brings us to Jesus' final priority. It had to do with His view of the law.

Have you ever considered that almost all human institutions end up constructing terribly complex laws? It's as if authorities believe that very complex laws are needed to direct the lives of very simple people.

Jesus had a different view. He seemed to recognize that people are inherently complex. His law was simple; there was only one: Love. "You shall love the Lord, your God, with all your heart, with all your being, with all your strength, and with all your mind, and your neighbor as yourself." (Luke 10:27) Jesus joined together what had previously been separate laws dealing with love of God and love of neighbor. From his viewpoint, this one resulting law contained all previous laws and all the prophets had said. It was the way He lived His life. He called those around Him to do the same, despite the problems and difficulties they encountered.

On the surface, just one law may sound like a wonderful thing. It really isn't. We are used to a myriad of laws, allowing us to obey the ones we want to and conveniently ignore others. It allows us to pick and choose. But just one law is a far different matter. There is no way to avoid it. If you allow yourself, thinking about it can even be downright scary. Love. Love those you want to love, love those you don't want to love—the driver who cuts you off, the loved one who rejects you, the terrorist who wants to kill you. Yes, love even your enemies. Take up your problems and imperfections, whatever they may be, and follow Jesus, living as He did: judge not, condemn not, forgive, and share. Lead by serving. Accept, as Jesus did, the world as it is, rather than as you would have it. Accept that in the final analysis, the only person you can change is yourself.

The journey Jesus calls us to is an inward one. The law of love is a call to open ourselves to the transforming power of love, to accept the reality that only as we change ourselves will the world around us change.

Finally, any discussion of Jesus' priorities must include the matter of Jesus' promise. Jesus promised many things in the Gospels, but I think that in the end, they all added up to just one: "Whoever receives me receives the one who sent me." (Matthew 10:40) Whoever accepts Jesus' priorities receives the one who sent Him. Those who are willing to recognize the importance of God in their lives, to accept that they are imperfect and in need of healing, and to open themselves to the transforming power of love, will gain everything. They will experience the healing of past hurts, joy and a sense of peace in this world, and union with the Divine in the next. Forever.

*Note: Shortly before preparing this reflection, I happened to listen to Father Richard Rohr's audiotape "Hearing the Wisdom of Jesus." I am sure that many of my ideas in this reflection were influenced by Father Rohr's talk.*

# *Fear*

*In his verse "Out of Order," Andre Awe describes his reactions when he comes upon the scene of a young mother trying to explain to her four-year-old boy that a popcorn machine cannot give out its contents.*

*"You can't get the popcorn, child, the machine is out of order. See, there is a sign on the machine."*

*But he didn't understand. After all, he had the desire, and he had money, and he could see popcorn in the machine. And yet somehow, somewhere, something was wrong because he couldn't get the popcorn.*

*The boy walked back with his mother, and he wanted to cry.*

*And Lord, I too feel like weeping, weeping for people who have become locked-in, jammed, broken machines, filled with goodness that other people need and want and yet will never come to enjoy, because somehow, somewhere something has gone wrong inside." (1)*

I would like to talk about fear.

There are healthy forms of fear. When I approach a crosswalk on a busy street, I make sure there are no cars coming before I start across. I am *afraid* of what might happen to me if I were to be hit by a speeding car. When I light a burner on a gas stove, I make sure I don't get too close. If I do, the pain teaches me to keep my distance in the future. Healthy fear helps protect me from danger.

Scripture, particularly the Old Testament, encourages us to "fear the Lord," meaning to show profound respect or be filled with a great sense of awe. I think this kind of fear enhances one's spiritual growth. Fear can also help us when our basic needs for food, shelter, and security are not being met. A healthy fear prompts us to take action to meet these needs.

Fear becomes unhealthy when we allow it to grow to the point where it actually limits our ability to meet our basic needs. The most common arena in which we all let this happen is in matters related to love, particularly the threatened loss of love. I think this is true because the need to love and to be loved is so fundamental in our make-up. We literally can't live without it.

When we think someone we care for doesn't care for us, we feel rejected. Rejection is painful. Anyone over the age of twelve, probably younger, can attest to this fact. We have all had lost loves. We have all felt the pain of rejection. As a result, we have all dealt with unhealthy fear.

Our first reaction is similar to how we would deal with a busy street or a hot stove. We become more tentative. We don't want to get burned again. We stop telling others how we really feel or who we really are. We then wonder why no one understands us. To protect ourselves further, we create superficial ways of dealing with those around us. These are called masks because they hide our true feelings, often to the point where even we aren't sure who we really are. To some extent, we all have masks: feigned indifference, righteous indignation, systemic pessimism, the macho man, the suffering saint, the comic, the one in control, and "I'm not good enough" are but a few examples. Whether we like it or not, almost all of us live with the fear that if you really knew me, you wouldn't like me.

If unhealthy fear is allowed to grow, a vicious cycle begins. As we shut others out, they find us still less attractive. We become increasingly focused on our discomfort. Maybe we really are unlovable. We become more sensitive to potential slights, sharing even less of ourselves, waiting for others to change. Since depending on another for one's happiness is always a fool's errand, our expectations are rarely, if ever met. As the fear grows, we withdraw even further behind our masks. We become self-centered. Eventually, we stop trying, and when we do, we become locked-in, jammed, broken.

Most of us have gotten so used to living with fear that we aren't even aware of its existence. We think life is filled with things. Busy-ness and superficiality are all there is. We don't realize that we are shutting ourselves off from fully developed relationships, and as a result, the ability to experience life fully. The pattern I have described may vary, but the results almost never do. Recognizing unhealthy fear and dealing with it is very important.

Jesus deals with fear in Mark's Gospel passage that describes His healing of a synagogue official's daughter. The official is faced with the threatened loss of love—his daughter is dying. We are that synagogue official.

Jesus' advice is simple and direct. "Do not be afraid; just have faith." (Mark 5:36)

*Do not be afraid*: Face the reality that you are dealing with fear.

*Just have faith:* Open yourself to love. Faith is openness to God. God is love. All love is from God. If this is true, then faith is openness to love—the willingness to accept the reality that we are lovable because we are loved. God created each of us as a unique, special gift because He loves each of us unconditionally. He made us lovable.

Fear and faith are mutually exclusive. Fear closes us down. Faith calls us to openness. Fear destroys. Faith builds up. With faith, we can accept that we are *always* loved. When we replace fear with faith, we begin to see how God brings goodness from every situation in life, even the threatened loss of a loved one.

It sounds so simple, but can it be true? Why not try it? Start every day by looking in the mirror and saying, "God loves me, just the way I am. I am always loved. I am lovable. It is good to be me." What have you to lose, other than a few minutes and possibly an entire future of life half-lived?

These are nice thoughts, but won't there still be times when it seems no one cares? Like the large crowd following Jesus to the synagogue official's home after hearing his daughter had died, we say to ourselves, "Why bother...love has died. No one cares what happens to me." But God never gives up on you. Like Jesus in the Gospel, God is always seeking you out, wherever you may be, despite your ridicule, your weeping, or your wailing. And if you take time to listen, you may just hear God saying, "Why all this commotion?" and then, "My little one, I say to you, arise! Arise, live, for you are loved."

On July 4th we celebrate Independence Day. We celebrate the resolve of our forefathers to be free. We, too, can resolve to be free—free of fear, free to live as God intended. As one of our past presidents so aptly put it, "We have nothing to fear but fear itself." (2)

Live. Love. Do not be afraid; just have faith.

1. John Powell, *Seasons of the Heart,* p. 104
2. Franklin Roosevelt

# *Faith*

The following notice appeared in a church bulletin:

> *The Women's Guild flea market sale will be held on the second Saturday of next month. Anything worth selling will be gratefully accepted. Please, ladies, look around your households for objects you may no longer want to keep but would rather sell than throw out. Don't forget to bring your husbands.*

Misunderstandings occur all the time, even when we think we are being perfectly clear in what we are trying to communicate.

Jesus spent most of His adult ministry communicating. The simple stories He told were designed to help people understand and remember relatively sophisticated or unfamiliar notions. Yet in at least one instance, I completely missed the point.

For years I misunderstood the parable about the sower casting seed upon different kinds of ground. Every time I heard it, I felt guilty. I felt as if there was something I wasn't doing right, or hard enough, or with sufficient zeal. Maybe it was my

Catholic upbringing—Catholics, and perhaps most Christians of my age group, are capable of feeling guilty at the slightest provocation. "Path," "rocky ground," and "thorns" seemed to apply to my inability even to remember, let alone adhere to, the various rules and teachings of my church. Words like "scorched," "withered," and "choked" sounded like well-deserved punishment for my shortcomings.

The problem with misunderstanding is not just that we miss what the speaker is trying to tell us; we are also affected by what we think the message is. A God perceived as threatening produces feelings of guilt. Who wants to be close to someone threatening? Better to keep him at arm's length. This leads to a mental shrugging of shoulders when we hear that God loves us and that Jesus came to tell us the Good News.

Fortunately, I had the opportunity to correct my misunderstanding, and I learned a lesson. Once I realized what Jesus was saying in this parable, I vowed I would use the following principle whenever I read the Gospels: If it doesn't strike me as good news, then I don't understand it!

Jesus' parable about the sower provides good news indeed. First, it tells us something about the *nature of God.* If we wanted to provide a title for this parable, a leading candidate would have to be "The Parable of the Sloppy Sower." Think about it. This guy spreads seed everywhere, indiscriminately. I think Jesus is telling us something. God seeks us out wherever we are. He is providing us with the "seed" of His love. We call it grace. We don't earn this love. We don't even earn his attention, yet there is no place we can go where He will not be, calling us into a love relationship. From personal experience, I know this is sometimes hard to believe, but it is true.

And He is not going to stop until He succeeds.

> Thus says the LORD:
>     Just as from the heavens
>       the rain and snow come down
>     and do not return there
>       till they have watered the earth,
>       making it fertile and fruitful
>     giving seed to the one who sows
>       and bread to the one who eats,
>     so shall my word be
>       that goes forth from my mouth;
>     my word shall not return to me void,
>       but shall do my will,
>     achieving the end for which I sent it.

> —Isaiah 55:10-11

The parable of the sower is also a story about the *nature of faith*. The earth is inert, incapable of producing results without some catalyst. In the parable of the sower, Jesus describes the ability of different kinds of soil to respond to seed. Think of the path, rocky ground, and thorny and rich soils as varying degrees of openness. Faith, at its core, is openness, a willingness to open ourselves to the reality we call God. It is based on the realization God can do for us what we cannot do by ourselves. It involves a conscious decision to let the seed of His grace bear fruit in our lives.

Too often we confuse the words "faith" and "belief." When we say Catholic or Methodist or Jewish "faith," we really mean belief in the doctrines of a particular faith tradition. True faith allows such belief to flourish, just like the seed sown in rich soil. Adherence to specific religious beliefs in the absence of faith is like seed sown on rocky ground. No matter how hard we try, we can't make it on our own. The root system of faith will be too weak to support growth.

A common feature of Jesus' healing miracles was His reference to faith, yet it was impossible for some of those healed to know who or what Jesus was. For example, Jesus encountered a centurion during a visit to Capernaum. I think it is fair to assume that the centurion knew very little about Jesus as the Messiah or the Jewish God in general. Yet after they had discussed healing the centurion's servant, Jesus remarked, "Amen, I say to you, in no one in Israel have I found such faith." (Matthew 8:10) A servant was healed because a centurion was open to Jesus' healing power. He was willing to have faith.

Finally, the parable of the sower is a story about the *benefits of faith*. "…Some seed fell on rich soil, and produced fruit, a hundred or sixty or thirtyfold." (Matthew 13:8) When we open ourselves to the reality of God, we become more. Healing takes place. Liberated from ungrounded fears, we "share in the glorious freedom of the children of God." (Romans 8:21) We live with the certainty we are never alone. Our beliefs, in ourselves and in our God, are firmly rooted and can grow. We become fruitful.

God promises that He will search us out, wherever we are. God promises we will become more, if we are willing to open ourselves to Him. And as we are willing to receive more, more will be given. These are the gifts from a God of Good News.

Whoever has ears ought to hear.

# *Gifts*

A paradox involves a statement that we are told is true, but seems to fly in the face of common sense. I have often wondered about certain paradoxes. One that used to be particularly bothersome concerns the nature of God. Our faith tradition tells us that God is good, yet we know from experience that life often isn't.

In theory, God, in His goodness, created us in His image. In doing so, He made each of us a unique reflection of His goodness. There is no one in the whole world just like you or me. While we are similar in many ways, science tends to confirm this uniqueness. It can now be demonstrated that things like our hair, eyes, voice, and fingerprints are all one of a kind. Yet, it still seems hard to believe that in all the endless number of worlds God could have created, He chose to create this one, with you and me in it, just the way we are. The world just wouldn't be the same without us. We are God's gifts.

If this is true, if God went to the trouble to create a world filled with his gifts, why is life so difficult? From personal experience, we know that life is filled with challenges, problems, and disappointments. God is good; life is difficult. How can this be?

After a great deal of reflection, I decided that a good part of the answer to this question lies in the nature of gifts. The dictionary provides us with two definitions for the word "gift." One is what we usually think of: "The voluntary transfer of something from one person to another without compensation." (1) In this sense we are truly gifts. God created us as we are. He gave us the gift of life. And we have received his gift without needing to promise or do anything in return.

The second definition is one we often overlook: "A notable capacity or talent." (2) In creating us, God gave us gifts—capacities or talents—to use as we choose. Some are common, some unique.

My wife and I have four children. They all have their own unique gifts: the ability to cook, to lead, to teach, to make others comfortable. They also share other talents in common, most notably their ability to care.

Everyone has such gifts, although it is easier to see them in others than in ourselves. What makes these gifts so interesting is that we feel good when we use them. We feel affirmed. Perhaps more importantly, gifts increase as they are used. They become greater. When I am patient with others, I become more patient with myself. As I forgive others, I come to know I am forgiven. The more I learn to laugh, the more it seems that even the problems and challenges of life have their humorous sides. Gifts grow as they are used. Sadly, the opposite is also true.

Our God has given us the gifts we need to live life fully, including the ability to deal with life's problems and inevitable disappointments. All too often, we just don't use the gifts we have been given. Maybe the answer to our apparent paradox is simple: God is good; we make life difficult.

Unfortunately, most of us have a hard time believing that we are special or have gifts. Even the apostles did.

We think of the apostles as extraordinary people. Yet if we look closely, we are struck by just how ordinary they were. The group was composed of some not-very-competent fishermen, including one who kept saying the wrong thing at the wrong time. Two of the apostles appeared to be Mama's boys, one was so stubborn he wouldn't believe anything without actually seeing it, and one collected taxes for the hated Romans. As a group, they viewed themselves as so ordinary that they couldn't seem to understand what Jesus was telling them. More often than not, they missed the point He was making. They spent much of their time arguing about who was most important, and when the real crisis occurred, almost all turned out to be cowards. In spite of that, Jesus loved them and encouraged them to use their gifts. Thankfully they did, and as a result, ordinary men became extraordinary.

In Mark's Gospel, as well as in Matthew's and Luke's, Jesus sends the apostles on a journey. In doing so, He tells them they have authority over unclean spirits. He also gives them some very interesting advice.

First, He tells them to take almost nothing with them—no food, no sack, no money, no second tunic. By doing so, He is reminding them that they already have within them the gifts they need to be successful on their journey.

Next, He tells them to not measure success based on how other people react to them. No one can control how another deals with life. We can only control what we do. How often do we allow ourselves to believe that our happiness depends on what another person does or doesn't do? But Jesus knew. If you are not welcomed or listened to, shake the dust from your feet and get on with your life.

Finally, Jesus wants the apostles to share. He sends them two-by-two, because every journey is better when shared with another. And He clearly wants them to use their authority over unclean spirits to drive out demons and cure people. Sharing gifts is the reason for the journey.

You are on a journey called life.
Think of it as a process.

The more you engage in life by sharing your gifts,
the more life will give you in return.

Your happiness does not depend on another,
For you have authority over unclean spirits.

Our God is a God of goodness.
You are His reflection,

And the world
just wouldn't be the same
without you.

1. *Webster's New Collegiate Dictionary*, p. 484
2. *Webster's New Collegiate Dictionary*, p. 484

# *Christian*

Sometimes I wonder if I'm missing something important. The feeling is an uncomfortable one, roughly similar to taking a long trip and part way through, wondering whether or not my directions are correct.

The last time I started thinking this way was right after a friend had described Christianity as a "lifestyle" rather than a set of beliefs. *A lifestyle*, I thought. Using this criterion, am I a Christian? If Jesus happened to reappear in human form, would He recognize me as one of His followers? Perhaps you have wondered the same thing at some point.

As I am often prone to do when I have a question that bothers me, I started asking around for a book that might help. In this case, the book recommended to me was called *On Being a Christian*, by Hans Küng. I was told that Hans Küng was quite an authority on the question of Christian lifestyle. I was pleased to find the book both highly readable and thought-provoking.

At the risk of doing an injustice to the breadth and depth of the book, Küng's basic premise is that being a Christian is being radical. The word "radical" has the unfortunate connotation of danger or violence. Being radical in the sense we are using it here means only a willingness to depart from normal everyday behavior. Our religious beliefs, our attempts to follow the teachings and rules of our church, and even our willingness to attend various liturgical services are important, but they are secondary to a willingness to be radical—to be radical in the way in which we care.

One of the unique things Jesus did was to take two of the primary ideas from Jewish scripture and make them one. In His view, the commandment to love God with all your heart, all your being, all your strength, and all your mind was intimately connected to loving your neighbor as yourself. We love God by loving our neighbor. A stronger way of saying this would be to say that love of God is not possible without love of neighbor.

This does not mean that we must like everyone. As Martin Luther King once said, "I give thanks God only asked me to love my neighbor. It would be hard to like someone who is trying to burn down your home." What it does mean is Jesus taught that God is *our* Father, our common Father. This means I must accept *you* as my brother or my sister—whether you are a friend, an enemy, or someone I don't even know.

I accept you as my brother or sister by being willing to feel what you are feeling when you are in need. This is one of the things meant by "loving your neighbor as yourself." When I let myself feel as you feel, I can't help but reach out and try to heal what is hurt, asking for nothing more than that you feel better.

Feeling as another feels, reaching out to heal, and asking nothing in return—that was the pattern of Jesus' healing miracles. We call it "compassion." The cornerstone of being a Christian is a radical willingness to care—to care with passion.

The parable of the good Samaritan is one of the best-known stories from the Bible. It has all the elements of a great tale. There is danger: a road where robbers can attack you. There is tragedy: the helpless traveler is stripped, beaten, and left half dead. There is suspense: will help arrive in time? There is even the unexpected: a priest and a Levite—religious leaders of God's chosen people—rush by. The Samaritan, viewed with disdain by Jews because they believed Samaritans *weren't* part of God's chosen people, not only stops, but goes out of his way to help the traveler.

Finally, there is surprise. The story never answers the question "Who is my neighbor?" Instead, Jesus poses a different question. "Who is the good neighbor?" The answer is, of course, the one who is "moved with compassion at the sight" (Luke 10:33) of someone in need. The one who is willing to care, to reach out to try and heal, asking nothing in return but the well-being of the one in need—the Christian. It is almost as if Jesus is saying that if you are not willing to care, answering the question "Who is my neighbor?" is a waste of time. If you are willing to care, you already know the answer.

One final thought. Who do you think you are in the story? Most of us answer by saying we are the priest or the Levite, passing by those in need. While there is truth in this answer, I would like to suggest another.

Life is a journey—
Often challenging,
sometimes dangerous,
always a journey.

Too often
we find ourselves
alone,
robbed of what we cherish,
stripped of hope,
Feeling half dead,
Wondering,
will help
arrive in time?

Fortunately,
God is
the original good neighbor.
Caring deeply,
feeling as we feel,
trying to heal,

asking only
that we
go
and do the same.

# *Kingdom*

Some time ago, my wife and I were driving down to Florida from our home in New Hampshire. We enjoy the sense of togetherness that comes when we make a long trip by car. We were on a large divided highway when I noticed an object on the road in front of us; it was a moving object. It was a turtle, slowly plodding its way across the road. Whenever a car sped by, it would stop and hunker down inside its shell. Then, when the danger passed, off it would go again. It was as if it knew it would be OK if it just got to the other side of the road.

I started to think about that turtle. It may have been just the monotony of highway driving, but the thought struck me: at least in one way I was like that turtle, trying to get from here to there, in search of something *better*. When problems occurred, I would hunker down for a while, but sooner or later, off I would go again, searching for...something. The more I thought about it, the more I realized much of my life had been spent *searching*. Maybe I was really like that turtle. "What a crazy idea," I mused, and left the thought to die.

But it wouldn't. So I mentioned it to a friend a few weeks later. His reaction was interesting. "Doesn't surprise me. We all spend a good part of our lives searching—for a better job, a better place to live, a better relationship, a better life."

It's as if there is an empty spot within each of us, something missing. And, sensing we are incomplete, we look for whatever it is we think will bring completeness. How often have we thought, in one way or another,

If I can just get this thing,
or
if that person will just do what I want,
or
if I can just accomplish that task,
or
if I can just get to the other side of the highway,

I'll be happy.

While the object of our search may vary, the search itself continues.

What is it we are after? Specifics vary from individual to individual, but in the final analysis this "better life" seems to have something to do with our need for acceptance—our need to know we are loved. Most of us don't come close to using our full capabilities, to realizing our ultimate potential. In my opinion, the most common reason for failing to utilize our

God-given gifts—in fact, the underlying cause of most of our problems—is a lack of sufficient self-esteem. We are not sure we are loved, so we continue to search.

In the Gospels, Jesus talks about searching. Two of his parables describe the search for items of great value: a hidden treasure and priceless pearls. It's as if Jesus knows that we spend much of our life searching for something of great value.

We are told this "something of great value" is the kingdom of heaven. What is this kingdom? What makes it so precious?

Let me suggest an answer to both questions. If our God is a God of love and the kingdom is the environment, place, dimension, or state of being where God reigns, then the kingdom of heaven is the fulfillment of God's love. It is the certainty, and therefore the acceptance that I am loved unconditionally. I am complete. I am able to accept fully the goodness that is me, the goodness of God, of others, of all God's creation. No wonder Jesus focuses on the incredible joy in finding this kingdom: "…out of joy goes and sells all he has and buys that field." (Matthew 13:46) Imagine how you felt the last time you realized someone important to you truly cared for you. The feeling of joy: I am loved! I am special!

But why is this kingdom hidden? Why must we search?

Personally, I don't subscribe to the reason I'm often given: "That's *after* we die. This life is where we *earn* the right to get there." While Jesus did say the full kingdom would come at some undefined point in the future, He also said, "The kingdom of heaven is at hand." (Matthew 4:17)

No, I believe the kingdom seems hidden because we spend most of our time searching for the wrong things. Like Solomon, we need help recognizing right from wrong. In this case, what is right is priceless, and therein lies the rub.

We are searching for the wrong things because we have a hard time accepting that which is so priceless—that I am good, you are good, and God's creation is good. As the musician Gregory Norbet wrote, "There is a pearl of great price within you. It is your hidden self, where God abides, the seed of all goodness and love, the power of all that is wholesome and life-giving." (1)

Look for God's goodness—in yourself…in others…in all the situations of your life…even, or maybe I should say *especially*, in the problems of life. God may not cause your problems, but He will always bring good from them if you let Him.

Seek and you shall find
Your hidden treasure, your priceless pearl.

Believe the good news:
The reign of God is at hand.

1. Gregory Norbet, "There Is a Pearl"

# *Miracles*

Several summers ago I hurt my right shoulder so badly I could not lift my arm. I think I did it while mowing our fields in New Hampshire, but I am not sure. What I was sure about was the doctor's diagnosis: I had hurt my rotator cuff and would not be able to use my right arm for up to six months. Since I had plans to go fly-fishing with my son in less than a week, the answer was obvious—I needed a miracle!

This revelation may not have done much good for my shoulder, but it did help in another arena. It gave me an idea for this reflection, particularly when I discovered that seemingly by coincidence, the Gospel for the following Sunday dealt with one of Jesus' miracles: feeding five thousand people with five barley loaves and two fish.

Have you ever been a part of or witnessed a miracle? Most of us answer this question with something like, "Of course not."

Why do we answer this way? The scriptures are filled with miracles, yet almost none of us believe we have ever been part of one. Is it because miracles stopped happening a long time ago? Or as some of us may have wondered, did they ever happen at all?

One definition of a miracle is this: an unexpected and usually unearned experience, which in satisfying some need allows one to live more fully. In the Gospel healing miracles, the people being healed neither expected nor had done anything to earn the gift they received. Clearly, healing satisfied some basic need: the need to hear, to see, to be free from disease, or to resume living. And once healed, the individuals involved were obviously able to live life more fully.

In the miracle of the loaves and fishes, the five thousand who came to listen to Jesus weren't expecting a free lunch and hadn't done anything to earn it; they hadn't even thought to bring anything along themselves. The need satisfied was their hunger, and those who witnessed the miracle were blessed with the recognition that they were part of something special.

Miracles, once defined, don't seem that mysterious.

The scriptures are clear on what conditions need to be present for a miracle to occur. First, God must be willing to do something. God is the source of all miracles. In the story of the loaves and the fishes, Jesus recognizes a problem (hungry people) and does something about it (feeds them). The twelve baskets of leftover fragments remind us of how abundant God's goodness is.

Isn't this still true? God didn't decide to stop loving humanity two thousand years ago, did He? No, the first condition for miracles still seems to be in place.

The only other condition for a miracle to occur is for the people involved to show up. All those who were healed by Jesus, or their representatives, came into His presence. They knew why they were there. The five thousand all came to hear Jesus. They showed up. For miracles to occur, we need to show up. God seems to be very particular on this point. I think it has something to do with free will. And this may be where the problem lies.

My image of the miracle of the loaves and fishes may be different from yours. I think most of the people there reacted differently from what is implied by the Gospel author. While some small number recognized what really happened, I think the reason Jesus was able to leave so easily was that most of those present failed to see anything special in the events of the day. In a sense, they failed to show up.

Some missed the miracle because they simply refused to believe that miracles were possible. Most of the time you can't see what you will not believe. Sitting on the grassy slope, they probably reacted something like this: "You say He made all these appear? You gotta be kidding! That's just not possible. No one's going to make a fool outta me. By the way, pass me another loaf."

Then there were the people in attendance who took miracles for granted: "George, are we having loaves and fishes again? That's the third time this week!"

Finally, there were those who were so absorbed in themselves that they weren't going to notice anything around them. You know the kind I mean. "I came all this way just to hear this guy. You'd think whoever's providing the food would be a little more considerate and at least heat the fish!"

While these examples may seem humorous, can't we see a little of ourselves in them? Whether we just won't believe in the possibility of miracles, take them for granted, or are too absorbed in our own problems to bother noticing, miracles aren't real because we won't let them be. We have come up with a name so we don't even have to use the word. We call them "coincidences."

It is a real tragedy when we fail to recognize the miracles occurring in our lives. If I truly believe that God has acted in my life to satisfy some need of mine, God becomes real. No longer is He something I experience second hand through what I read or through what others tell me. I know, in the core of my being, that I am special because God cares enough to help me live life more fully. I know God is blessing me, helping me experience happiness. I no longer just say "God bless you." I can say, "God blesses me." For all this to be true, all I have to do is look!

I would like to tell you about two miracles in my life. Not because they are particularly unique, but in the hope that they will help you identify the miracles in your own lives. The key is to look for times when you have felt blessed (living life more fully), and then see if there was some coincidence (an unexpected and often unearned occurrence) involved. As a friend of mine says, "There is no such thing as a coincidence."

Sometimes miracles affect a readily identified need. Over ten years ago I learned that I had prostate cancer. An apparently successful operation was followed by a reemergence of the disease. I then tried radiation, with the same result. The next procedure recommended by my doctor was not particularly attractive; it would only slow the spread of cancer with no possibility of a cure. In addition, there was the strong possibility I would experience negative side effects.

At this point, my brother started asking me to meet with someone he thought might be able to help. I was so enmeshed in self-pity I didn't want to be bothered. I think the only reason I finally agreed was to stop his badgering. It has since occurred to me that Jesus may have blinded Paul because it was the only way he could get his attention.

By coincidence, when I did meet my brother's friend, he gave me a book. By coincidence, the book contained a chapter on a then-largely-unknown herbal remedy, which, because I felt I had nothing to lose, I decided to start taking. Within sixty days my cancer was gone. Three years later, it shows no sign of reemergence. I feel that I have a new lease on life. I feel blessed.

Sometimes miracles address a need we aren't even aware of. Shortly after college, I went to Boston to make my fortune. Once there, a co-worker fixed me up with a friend named Frannie Vincent. Frannie was on the verge of getting engaged, but her boyfriend, a naval officer, had just left for a six-month cruise. Since I knew I could not afford a serious relationship, meeting Frannie seemed like a wonderful coincidence…someone I could enjoy without any danger of entanglement.

Nine months later, we were married. In a way I had never thought of, I found my fortune. This year we celebrated our forty-second anniversary. She is my best friend. She has given depth and color and substance to my life. I am truly blessed.

Miracles happen.

God's way
of helping us
become more than we were.

Look for the miracles in your life.
Believe and you will see
God's goodness brought to fulfillment.

# *Diversity*

Have you ever thought about diversity—the mystery of being different? Diversity is a mystery because it is paradoxical. Diversity enriches our lives, yet at the same time, it makes us uncomfortable.

Imagine for a moment what the world would be like if there were only one color. We actually are able to perceive over one million colors. What a gift! Wouldn't life be dull if there were only one? At times I am saddened when I think of the number of people I know who see only the grays in life.

What if there were only one note of music? This seems preposterous, but wouldn't we lose a great deal if it were so? Color and music are just two examples of how diversity enriches our lives.

God's creation contains countless gifts which enhance our lives if and when we allow them to touch us. I am sure you can think of times in your own life when you found yourself in an unfamiliar environment and afterwards marveled at what you had gained from the experience. Diversity enriches our lives because it expands and deepens the beauty of life. Of course, just as in the case of color and music, differences must be harmonized to take on real meaning.

Diversity also has the potential to make us uncomfortable. I think this is rooted in our instinctive need for security—to feel safe. As with all instincts, there is good reason for this need, but it can be overdone. Let me give you an example. One way we feel safe is to associate with others like ourselves. Over time, there is a tendency to start thinking of our group as better than others and of everyone else as inferior. The result is an uncomfortable feeling when we encounter those who are different, whether the differences are based on family, race, religion, culture, or a simple lack of familiarity. Being uncomfortable results from a sense of insecurity.

Unfortunately, to a greater or lesser extent, almost all human groupings, ranging from the nation state to the nuclear family, tend to follow this pattern. The history of almost every religion illustrates this unfortunate truth.

The Gospel account of Jesus' encounter with the Canaanite woman in Tyre deals with diversity. The Canaanites were considered ancestral enemies of the Jewish people. In addition, Jewish law prohibited interchange with anyone other than another Jew. In other words, Jesus encounters someone who is different while he is in an unfriendly place.

To understand the interchange between the two, we must remember that Jesus was both divine *and* human. We spend so much time focusing on Jesus' divinity that we sometimes forget that Jesus was also fully human.

Jesus' humanity shows in His reaction to the Canaanite woman. At first, Jesus does as He had been taught to do: He ignores her. "But Jesus did not say a word in answer to her." (Matthew 15:23) When we see someone different, isn't our first impulse to pretend that he or she simply does not exist? I don't know about you, but this is what I almost always do.

The Canaanite woman persists, to the point that the apostles plead with Jesus to deal with her. Jesus feels she is not His responsibility. "I was sent only to the lost sheep of the house of Israel." (Matthew 15:24) Sound familiar? How many times have we avoided someone in need by saying something like this: "I've got my family to care for; why doesn't the government do something about that?"

Finally, when the woman simply won't go away, Jesus becomes irritated and says, "It is not right to take the food of the children and throw it to the dogs." (Matthew 15:26) When all else fails, our response tends to be that someone different does not deserve our attention.

Pretending someone doesn't exist, rationalizing responsibility, and thinking that another is undeserving are very common reactions to diversity. Such feelings, in and of themselves, are neither right nor wrong. It is how we act on our feelings towards others that is important.

The Canaanite woman provides an interesting example of how to benefit from diversity. She is open to the good will of a stranger, even someone very different from herself. She is non-judgmental, avoiding a negative reaction when initially rebuffed. She is persistent, and even willing to use a little humor. "Even the dogs eat the scraps that fall from the table of their masters." (Matthew 15:27)

When faced with this openness, Jesus finally decides what action He will take. "Let it be done for you as you wish." (Matthew 15:28) Jesus uses His gift of healing, and He does so without condition. Jesus reaches out and shares, even though He is in foreign territory and confronted by a person who is supposed to be an enemy.

Diversity is a mystery, based on the contrast between its benefits and the reaction it often elicits. It is also a mystery because its value depends upon the choices we make—not on how we initially feel, but on the action we take. Are we willing to share ourselves in a complementary way—whether by our openness, persistence, sense of humor, or healing—to expel the demons of insecurity? We all have these gifts. Their use leads to life more richly lived. I think this is one of the reasons Jesus promised that whenever we give, we shall receive more than we have given.

Diversity is a gift,
fundamental to God's creation.

Avoiding diversity diminishes us
and belittles the greatness of our God.

Embracing diversity enriches us,
enhancing the fabric of our lives,
helping us experience the Divine.

# *Will Power*

Right versus wrong. Do right…avoid wrong.

This simple admonition is fundamental to living. Whether it is rules from our parents, commandments from our religion, or laws and customs from our culture, it seems we always have some force in our lives reminding us to "Do right, avoid wrong. Do right…and be good. Do wrong and you will be sent to your room, to jail (social if not physical), or to hell."

In so many ways and by so many people we are told, "Do right, avoid wrong." And when we make mistakes (and we all do), it always seems as though there's someone—Mom and Dad at home, Aunt Millie from next door, or a teacher at school—telling us, "You don't have to be bad…you can do the right thing. It's just a matter of will power."

Unfortunately, it isn't quite that easy most of the time. Will power doesn't seem to be enough. Sometimes the "right thing" to do is obvious. But many times, for many reasons, it is not.

Saint Paul tells us, "Do not conform...to this age." (Romans 12:2) But it's hard not to. After all, everyone wants to fit in.

The Commandments say we should not kill another person. Obvious, it would appear. And yet, when my father was in great pain and appeared to be dying several years ago, the doctor suggested stopping the intravenous feeding. I wondered, "What is the right thing to do?"

Too often the words "Well, everyone does it!" turn a temptation into a good idea. Almost without our knowing it, the "right thing to do" becomes an almost insatiable desire to do what others think is acceptable. Just think of our preoccupation with material wealth, the abuse of our bodies through what we consume, how we treat the gift of our sexuality, or just the simple exclusion of another person from our affection.

Then there are the times when, like Saint Peter, we find it so easy to rationalize if doing the right thing involves difficulty or the threat of pain. When Jesus announces that He must go through a period of suffering, Peter responds as we most likely would, "God forbid, Lord! No such thing shall ever happen to you." (Matthew 16:22)

Finally, too many of us pretend that doing what we think is right somehow earns God's protection from the problems of life. Next time you are in the midst of difficulty and want to scream, "Why me, God?" just remember His answer is probably "Why not you?" Life happens, problems and all. Believing anything else is not only wishful thinking, it helps us justify inaction when action is clearly called for.

All this said, it seems to me that the greatest difficulty in doing the right thing is this: we all have within us an instinctive desire to do right. This means that when we do something wrong, we make ourselves believe it isn't wrong at all. One of the messages of the Adam and Eve story is their motivation for eating the apple. Adam and Eve did not decide to upset God; they just wanted knowledge. They convinced themselves they were doing the right thing. All too often, you and I are Adam and Eve.

No, we don't seem to do a very good job on our own. It's not just a matter of will power. Or is it?

Scripture suggests a different kind of will power—the power of God's will, operating in our lives. To accept this notion, I think one has to accept three related ideas. First, God knows me better than anyone, even better than I know myself. Second, God knows what is right for me, better than anyone, even better than I do. Third, God wants my happiness more than anyone, even more than I do. Most people have a particularly difficult time accepting this last idea. God wants my happiness more than anyone, even more than I do. Enduring happiness is life lived fully. Life lived fully is God's will for us. Life lived fully is right.

Aren't sure? Try this little exercise. Keep track of how you feel a few hours or a few days after doing something. If you feel remorse, guilt, emptiness ("that wasn't such a big deal...why did I think that was so important?"), or, worse yet, can't even remember what you did—that's *your* will power. You are doing *your* thing. Jesus called it "wishing to save your own life."

On the other hand, if you feel good about what you did, know somehow you are better off, and can say to yourself, "Gee, that was the right thing to do," that's the power of God's will in your life. You and God are doing *His* thing. Jesus called it "losing your life for my sake."

But how do I know God's will *before* deciding what to do? Jesus suggested that we pray. Remember, it's not "my will be done" but "thy will be done." Pray and you will get an answer. Jesus promised, "Ask and it will be given to you...everyone who asks, receives." (Matthew 7:7-8) Then listen.

Sometimes the answer comes through what another person says to us—one of those little coincidences that seem to occur at precisely the right moment. Sometimes it will be intuition. As a friend of mine used to say, "Just do the next right thing." Often, it will be your conscience—that little voice with the idea that won't go away. Jeremiah called it "a fire burning in my heart." (Jeremiah 20:9)

And finally, practice. As you go through your day, think, "What would God want me to do?" After a while it will start to become second nature. Just as a gymnast becomes more graceful with practice, so with practice will you become more grace-filled.

Don't be surprised if you begin to feel like laughing more, sharing more, enjoying the small pleasures of life more. And please don't get discouraged. We all have crosses to bear. That's part of the mystery of life. The only question is whether we will carry them or they will bury us.

If we do our part, the goodness of God—God's will that we live life to the fullest—will never let us down.

And so, my brothers and sisters,

> Do not conform yourselves to this age
> but be transformed by the renewal of your mind,
> that you may discern what is the will of God,
> what is good and pleasing and perfect.

—Romans 12:2

# Fall

# *Choices*

We all make choices. We choose what we will do and not do, what we will be and not be, even what makes us happy and what makes us sad. Choices are important.

One thing we can be certain about when it comes to our choices is this: some won't be the right ones. That's part of life. The question is not whether we will be perfect—that's not possible—but whether we will learn from our mistakes.

One kind of choice we make involves saying one thing and thinking or doing another. You known what I mean. "Oh, I'm so sorry to hear Mrs. Jones is doing poorly," while at the very same time thinking, "Well, she's finally getting what she deserves."

This can be an uncomfortable subject for most of us, even though we all do it. Perhaps our discomfort arises from the fact that since we don't acknowledge the mistake at the time we make it, we are doomed to repeat it.

Personally, however, I think we don't like to talk about such behavior because it touches on a secret we all have: there are two of me. One is the me I present to you and the rest of the world, the "Everything's fine and I'm doing what you and the rest of the world expect me to do" me. Then there is the inner me, where I grapple with my fears and frailties and "Am I really lovable?" concerns.

While saying one thing and doing another is common to all of life's activities, it seems to be particularly prevalent in organized religion. In one of His parables, Jesus describes two brothers, both who say one thing and do another. The difference lies in what they choose to do. (Matthew 21:28-32) Actions speak louder than words.

Jesus uses this story to admonish the representatives of organized religion—the chief priests and elders—for what they have failed to do, contrasting their behavior unfavorably with that of far less reputable individuals like the tax collectors and prostitutes. I sense urgency in what Jesus is communicating. He seems to know something very basic that the religious leaders are missing. Maybe He is trying to communicate an important idea to us as well.

The fundamental theme of Christianity, and for that matter Judaism, is the supremacy of the love command. Jesus is calling for a radical choice on the part of all who hear Him, because love is a choice. Love as your Father loves. Love with forgiveness, generosity, and compassion. Love in a limitless way.

Loving in a limitless way isn't easy. It involves change, and change is hard. It involves sacrifice, because love isn't all joy and light. There are sad times as well, touched with loneliness and pain. Finally, when it comes right down to it, we are more comfortable with limiting laws than we are with limitless love. We like to know the extent of our responsibility. We want to quantify—church one day a week, prayer once a day, the call to my mother every weekend. We prefer to compartmentalize our affection.

Before we know it, we are caught in the cycle of doing things right, rather than doing the right things. We go through the motions. We say one thing and do another. All too often we are the chief priests and elders.

Yet God calls. In the Old Testament, Isaiah, Jeremiah, and Ezekiel all voice God's plea. "Is it my way that is unfair, or rather, are not your ways unfair?" (Ezekiel 18:25) In the New Testament, Saint Paul calls us to imitate Christ, assuming the same attitude as Christ, and Jesus the Christ leaves no doubt as to what His attitude is.

On the cross, dying for "the forgiveness of sins" (Matthew 26:29), He was still willing to say, "Father, forgive them, they know not what they do." (Luke 23:34)

When asked what the single greatest law is, Jesus names two: love of God, and love of neighbor. Love of neighbor is not possible without love of God. At the same time, love of God is not possible without love of neighbor.

As important as church attendance is, Jesus says that if on your way to church you remember a problem you have with a loved one, go to the loved one and heal your relationship *before* going to church.

Jesus performed healing miracles on the Sabbath, a violation of sacred law for the devout Jew. Yet heal on the Sabbath Jesus did, even though as in the case of the man who had had a withered hand all his life, Jesus could have waited until the next day. Actions speak louder than words. Actions with a sense of urgency speak loudest.

In Jesus' description of the final judgment, with the "goats" on his left and the "sheep" on his right, Jesus invites into his Father's kingdom those who reached out to the hungry, the lonely, the imprisoned. At times we are all hungry, lonely, or imprisoned. But to those who refuse to recognize Him in their neighbors, who say, "But, Lord, I went to church…I followed the rules…I just didn't recognize you…" Jesus says, in effect, "You missed the point."

The urgency of Jesus' message bothered me for a long time. Why was he so insistent? Then one day an image came to me—an image of my son when he was very young, just twenty-two months old. I was called back from vacation because he was in the hospital. When I entered his room, I found him in an oxygen tent, gasping for breath, trying to live, but not quite sure how to. I was overcome with emotion. An incredibly strong sense of urgency consumed me. I wanted to do *something*.

Like my son, maybe we are gasping for life, trying to live but not quite sure how to go about it. And maybe Jesus knows what will help.

Jesus calls us to forgive others because He knows that in doing so, we learn to forgive ourselves.

He calls us to choose generosity towards others, knowing that in doing so we will gain a sense of abundance in our own lives.

He calls us to choose a sense of compassion, knowing that in doing so we will gain a sense of connectedness, of community.

He calls us to choose love, limitless love with all its risks, because He knows that when we do so, we choose life, fully lived, fully loved.

And so we pray,

> Your ways, O LORD, make known to me;
> teach me your paths,

Guide me in your truth and teach me,
for you are God my savior.

—Psalm 25: 4-5

# *Meaning*

Recently, I had the opportunity to attend a meeting on various ways to promote spiritual renewal. The presenter was a sincere young man who seemed very knowledgeable. At one point during our discussion, he made an interesting comment. After describing a particular retreat format, he said, "This program appeals to young people because it answers the question 'What is the meaning of life?'" Inwardly chuckling, I thought to myself, *If this question is for young people, I must still be young.*

On the way home that night, the thought returned. Maybe I wasn't alone. Maybe we all wonder at some point in our lives, "What's the point? What's the purpose? Why am I going through all this?" I concluded that there isn't a single one of us who hasn't been through trying times, often accompanied by suffering, always accompanied by uncertainty. During these darker, drier times we find ourselves drawn to wondering, "What's the meaning of life?" And to make matters worse, right after we think we have it all figured out, something changes.

I would like to propose an answer. Not an original one, but an idea supplied by scripture. Life is a gift. Life is a gift because we are given the opportunity to grow into union with God. We are called to be divine.

Life is meaningful, to the extent that we take advantage of this opportunity, grateful during the highs, trusting during the lows. Life is meaningless to the extent that we don't. Life is meant to be a journey to completeness. Imagine a process, the process of growing up spiritually. I often think of this process as a call to holiness. Not holiness in the sense of ritual observance or adherence to church laws, but in the sense of becoming more complete, being made whole.

One thing Jesus did most often during his ministry was to help people become more complete. The most obvious examples are the healing miracles: restoring hearing, eyesight, or the use of limbs. For me, the significant aspect of these miracles was not the physical cure, but the healing of spirit that resulted from them. Those with disabling infirmities were excluded from the community because such infirmities signaled a presence of evil. They were deprived of human love, with the resulting loss of self-esteem. A physical cure allowed a more important form of healing: restoration to relationships within a community, to a sense of self-esteem, to a greater sense of wholeness.

We are called to wholeness.

Of course, nothing is as simple as it seems at first blush. Life has its problems and its challenges, regardless of some greater meaning, and these problems and challenges may be very traumatic at the time they occur. However, I think there is one overriding challenge and one overriding problem in living life in a meaningful way.

The challenge is this: we can't make it on our own. Since we are incomplete, we make mistakes, we take the wrong turns, we hit dead ends. And when something changes, giving us the opportunity to recover, we resist. All too often, our answer to the truism "No pain, no gain" is "No pain, thank you."

The challenge is that we can't make it on our own. The problem is that we think we can. Because we think we can make it all by ourselves, we tend to become like Bartimaeus in Mark's Gospel: *blind* (unable to see what's important) *as he sat* (stuck in the same place) *by the roadside* (watching life pass by), wondering about the meaning of life. (Mark 10:46-52)

Fortunately, there is a solution—one so obvious that you might think it was part of some plan. The call in "call to holiness" refers to God's promise to help, to lead us home, so to speak. What we need is the courage of Bartimaeus when he cried, "Jesus...have pity on me." (Mark 10:47)

Acknowledging that we need help is hard, particularly in a culture that places a premium on rugged individualism *and* the supposed advantages of easing discomfort with a bewildering array of substances poured into or onto our bodies. That's why I say the *courage* of Bartimaeus. "Many rebuked him, telling him to be silent." (Mark 10:48) Our culture rebukes the notion of asking God for his help. Think of the asking as a prayer—a prayer not from the head, but from the heart.

When the effort to ask is made, God always answers. "What do you want me to do for you?" (Mark 10:51)

Once again, the courage of Bartimaeus suggests an answer. Lord, I want not an easier life; I want not the resolution of one or another of life's many irritants. I want something I need desperately to live a meaningful life. I want to see what's important.

"Go your way; your faith has saved you." (Mark 10:52) Faith is a conscious decision to open oneself to God. Bartimaeus was open. His faith saved him. Openness to God's presence, his influence, his direction literally saves us, for it allows God to lead us.

Letting God direct our journey gives new and deeper meaning to the primary sign of our faith:; the cross. It no longer is a reminder of a past historical event, a reminder of death. The cross becomes a symbol for the promise that there will be a resurrection after every death, a new beginning for every ending. Letting God direct our journey means that the problems we encounter—all the times life seems capricious, or unfair, or tragic—are new opportunities for God to bring good, to help us become more complete as human beings, as hard as that may be to understand or accept at the time.

In fact, I sometimes wonder whether life's difficulties actually serve a purpose, prodding me to remember the real meaning of life.

Reinhold Niebuhr said it beautifully with this conclusion to his famous serenity prayer:

> …Trusting you will make all things right if I surrender to your will,
> So that I may be reasonably happy in this life
> and supremely happy with you forever in the next. (1)

God created us
in love.
In love,
He calls us to completeness.

Ask
and you shall receive.
Seek
and you will find.

Then
you will say,
"The Lord has done great things
for me,

for I
can see."

1. Reinhold Niebuhr, "The Serenity Prayer"

# Salvation

"Today salvation has come to this house." (Luke 19:9)

Have you ever thought about what salvation means? Obviously it is important to any believing Christian, but my guess is that a group of four people would come up with four different definitions. Is salvation a theological event, or a practical experience? Does it happen only once, and if so, when? Or does it occur over time? Does God save us, do we save ourselves, or is it something we help God do?

The concept of salvation can appear confusing for many reasons, including unfamiliar theological language, the oft-repeated phrase that Jesus saved us when He died, and Saint Paul's concentration on the link between Jesus' resurrection and our own. But I think most of the confusion lies in the difficulty we have in accepting two basic realities.

The first reality is that God is a personal God. He knew us before we were born, He loved us into being, and he is present and active in each moment of our lives. The vast majority of Christians I meet pay lip service to this idea, but they do not really believe it. The second reality is based on the first, and is almost as widely ignored. God created us in love so we could grow in love. We are lovable. It is good to be who we are, just the way we are.

Luke's account of Jesus' encounter with Zacchaeus deals with these two realities, and as a result, helps demystify the subject of salvation.

The process of salvation always begins with God's efforts to be part of our lives. "At that time, Jesus came to Jericho and intended to pass through the town." (Luke 19:1) The question is how do we respond to this effort? Like Zacchaeus, we have wealth, meaning that God blesses us in many ways. Like Zacchaeus, we are also incomplete. Often, we are short in stature, failing to live up to our own or others' expectations. We are also sinners—chief tax collectors who think only of taking from life without giving back. Unfortunately, our tendency to focus on our shortcomings usually overwhelms our sense of blessedness, leading to anxieties, worries, and a feeling of meaninglessness. Increasingly, we react to life, imprisoned by our insecurities—not all the time, to be sure, but enough to limit our ability to give and receive love.

Like Zacchaeus, we must make the effort to move beyond these insecurities to find the Divine in our lives. This effort may involve personal risk, climbing the proverbial tree and exposing our weaknesses to all. But this risk may be necessary if we are to rise above our normal view to find what's important in our lives.

It is the effort that counts. It is easy to forget that Jesus never asked for specific results. He said God would take care of the results because He loves us completely in our incompleteness. At the same time, Jesus told us in no uncertain terms that we must make the effort. He knew His Father would always be part of our lives, but could be truly present to us only when we made the effort to find Him. "Come down quickly, for today I must stay at your house." (Luke 19:5)

If I am willing to accept that Jesus truly wants to stay at my house, that God wants to be present in the most personal details of my life, then marvelous things will happen. A sense of joy results from finally accepting that God is with me, loves me just as I am, and will be with me always. "And he came down quickly and received him with great joy." (Luke 19:6)

Jesus frees me from feeling unworthy—the breeding ground for self-centered behavior. This acceptance empowers me to move beyond myself to more actively sharing myself with others. "Behold, half of my possessions, Lord, I shall give to the poor." (Luke 19:8) It also helps me make peace with the past. "If I have extorted anything from anyone, I shall repay it four times over." (Luke 19:8) I am free to live as I was meant to live, growing in connectedness to the world around me. I am free to grow in love, freely given and received, so I can grow into my final destiny—union with the God of life who is the source of all love.

*This is the process of salvation: making the effort so the Divine can free us to live more completely.* Salvation involves resurrection to new life. Jesus was raised from the dead. The same is promised for anyone willing to try. This is the promise of Christianity.

I know there are more theologically correct definitions of salvation. I know there are people with more eloquent explanations. But to me, it is fairly simple. Jesus came, by his own admission, to proclaim the good news that God is present, trying to break into my life, to bring His kingdom of love. The challenge for me is not learning another theology; the challenge for me is accepting that this good news may be true. Am I willing to risk exposure of my human failings as I open myself to the Divine? Am I willing to risk letting go of my way of doing things? Am I willing to make the effort? If I am, then I am convinced Jesus will say, "Today salvation has come to this house." (Luke 19:9)

# *Wisdom*

For some reason, many people think that wisdom is elusive. Whatever it might be, wisdom seems to be hard to find, and even harder to hold on to. If asked what it means, we would probably say something like this: "Wisdom involves exceptional insights on a broad range of subjects, accumulated over a long period of time." That's if we even thought the question was worth answering. Most of us think, "Only a few seem to have it; most don't, including me."

I think this view of wisdom, while prevalent, is dead wrong. Wisdom is not some elegant discipline involving exceptional insights. Wisdom is common sense. Wisdom does not involve a broad range of subjects. Wisdom is common sense, applied to the quality of our relationships—how we view ourselves, interact with each other, and deal with the Divine. Relationships determine how we feel about ourselves and the world around us, our sense of wholeness, and our level of hope. Wisdom is worth caring about.

Finally, wisdom is not the exclusive domain of some elite few. Wisdom is available to all who want it, "readily perceived by those who love her,/and found by those who seek her." (Wisdom 6:12) All it takes is trying. Wisdom is God's gift, the gift of His spirit, nudging us toward right relationships. And the gift is endless; once we start on this journey, there is always more to be given, if and when we are willing to receive it.

How to start? A friend gave me the following suggestions. He called them his philosophy for life. I like them because they are easy to remember and seem to contain great wisdom.

> Expect Nothing
> Do Your Work
> Celebrate

While working on my employer's "quality comes first" campaign in the late 1980s, I discovered an interesting fact. We were studying customer satisfaction in the hope of demonstrating that the most important factor in improving customer satisfaction is product quality. We were disappointed. The results of our study clearly showed that the most important factor in determining how satisfied a customer is with a product, service, *or* interaction with another human being is that person's expectation level. An example might help to demonstrate this.

Let's say I tell you I will come to your house for a visit at 11:00 AM. You expect me then, so when I arrive, you are satisfied. Results that match one's expectation level do not lead to feelings of euphoria, but rather to an almost neutral "Well, that's what I expected" feeling. Now, let's say I tell you I will come by your house for a visit at 11:00 AM, and around 9:00 AM you start thinking, "I really need to see Bill earlier." The more you think about it, the more you come to expect it. You might even call my house and leave a message, asking me to come earlier. Guess what happens when I arrive at 11:00 AM? You are disappointed because I did not meet your expectation level. The earlier you expected me, the unhappier you will be. Finally, same scenario, but around 9:00 AM you start thinking, "I know Bill; he never gets anywhere on time. I just know he will be late." I arrive at 11:00 AM, and you are pleased. I exceeded your expectation level. The more your expectation level is surpassed, the happier you will be.

"Expect nothing" is a catchy way of saying that to a very large extent, we control our own happiness. We determine how we feel about ourselves, others, and even our God. What a great gift! We have only one person to worry about, so to speak.

But you might be thinking, "expect nothing" sounds almost un-American. After all, aren't we taught that high expectations somehow lead to higher performance, better results, and greater fulfillment? I think the confusion has to do with mixing the appropriate activities of setting goals and trying our best with the often fatal attraction of anticipating a result so much that we start assuming a probable outcome: "I *expect* this to happen!"

The underlying premise of expecting is that we know what will happen. That's just not true. All we are doing is setting ourselves up to be disappointed.

Saint Paul's first letter to the Thessalonians and Jesus' parable about the ten virgins are both good examples of this. In both cases, the authors are dealing with expectation levels regarding Jesus' second coming. Paul's audience is convinced the end is upon them, and they are worried about their dead relatives. Will they miss the boat? The Gospel author is writing some years later. Jesus has not yet returned, and people are disappointed. Will He ever come? And so Matthew records Jesus' admonition not to let your guard down, for the bridegroom will come when you *least* expect it.

Wisdom recognizes that you cannot control the future—or other people, for that matter. You are not God. Expect nothing, and you shall not be disappointed. Instead, you will have built a solid foundation for feeling good about yourself and the world around you.

Do your work. Relationships take work. Love takes work. In the parable of the ten virgins in Matthew's Gospel, the difference between the wise and the foolish is the willingness to do what's necessary. Don't forget your flask of oil if you want to be included in the party. Relationships don't survive on last-minute pleas and reactive behavior. When it comes to all the little things that make a relationship special—listening to a loved one, forgiving a slight, saying you care when care is needed (and when isn't it?)—operate on the premise that "you know neither the day nor the hour" (Matthew 25:13) when you'll get another chance. Because you don't, and you may not.

Do your work, and increasingly you "shall...be free from care." (Wisdom 6:15)

Finally, it is no coincidence that Jesus uses a wedding celebration in His story about the ten virgins. He uses this theme quite often in the Gospels. There is great wisdom in celebrating. The willingness to do so is part of being fully alive. When we celebrate, we feel good about ourselves. We feel connected to others. We even experience a sense of the Divine, because celebration is what God calls us to do with Him, forever. We call this "heaven."

Celebrate what, you might ask? How about the gifts God tries to give you, including the gift of wisdom? How about the fact that God accepts you just the way you are? He has no false expectations. How about the fact that he works at helping you live life more fully by leading you to deeper, more meaningful relationships? And how about the fact that he celebrates when you are willing to recognize His presence? God celebrates when you do.

So expect nothing...do your work...and always remember to celebrate. And wisdom will be yours.

# *Endings*

The conclusion of our church year occurs near the end of November, at the same time the calendar year is almost over. It is a time of endings. Summer is but a memory. Fall is fading, with blowing leaves and frost-filled mornings. Winter's arrival seems just moments away. The Thanksgiving holiday announces that another year is ending.

End times are when we let go of what has been and face the uncertainty of what will be.

End times make us uneasy. The bigger the ending, the greater the dis-ease. A few years ago, we ended a whole millennium. Do you even remember how nervous people were? The number of survival books, movies, and TV features playing on our fears concerning this important end time? We even had a national crisis over a potential software problem called Y2K! Today, most people can't even remember what the acronym meant.

Perhaps this concern with end times helps explain why I used to be bothered by a question at this time of year. On the last Sunday of each church year we celebrate the feast of Christ the

King by reflecting on scripture readings relevant to the final end time. I used to spend very little time wondering what would happen to the world. My question was this: What will happen to me?

What will happen when I meet Jesus? What kind of king is He? We spend most of the church year talking about the love and compassion of Jesus. But on this feast day, we have this same Jesus telling some of us, "Depart from me, you accursed, into the eternal fire." (Matthew 25:41) Who will he tell? And why? Eternity is a long time.

What kind of king is Jesus? This is a more important question than many of us realize, because we tend to *become* our image of God, meaning that we tend to act the way we think God acts. If we think of God as loving and forgiving, we tend to adopt these traits. If we think of God as capricious or vengeful, we tend to be the same. I think our image of God has much to do with our deep-seated anxiety concerning end times in general. In the back of our minds, we are afraid God just might blow things up, so to speak.

Jesus describes the last judgment in Chapter 25 of Matthew's Gospel. Jesus is talking about the importance of sharing with those less fortunate. He uses an "end time" image to say that sharing our gifts with those in need is essential. Jesus even seems to be saying that sharing our gifts is more important than recognizing our God.

Yet, when we do finally meet Jesus on the day of our final judgment—a meeting the scriptures promise will actually take place—what will that meeting be like? What do *you* think? I know our behavior in this life will be a big factor, but doesn't it really depend on what kind of king Jesus is?

One view of our king could be called the "good sheep and bad goats" view. In this view, God is harsh and judgmental. When we meet with Jesus, the time for mercy is over. We will have had our chance. Jesus will say you are good or you are bad, *forever*. A few will go to eternal bliss, but most of us will suffer, *forever*. Pretty harsh, don't you think? If you aren't sure, imagine doing the same to one of your loved ones.

That's not all. In this view, the kingdom of heaven and the prison of hell are places—places a long way from here. They—and, as a result, our king—are distant, out of touch. Finally, Jesus is judgmental. He carries a long tally sheet. When you come before Him face to face He will pull it out, add up the pluses and minuses, and decide where you will spend eternity. Jesus the Judge: the harsh, distant Judge. Unfortunately, most of us carry around some form of "good sheep and bad goats" image of God.

The good news is that there is an alternative view, one popularized by Dennis, Sheila, and Matthew Linn. It is called the "good goats" image of Christ the King. (1) It is based on the reality that, in the scriptures, Jesus never judged anyone who tried to do the right thing. In fact, He seemed to spend most of His time helping those considered bad. He knew that almost all of us are neither good nor bad all the time.

We want to be good. We try to be good, to share with those who are hungry for affection or who are imprisoned by their loneliness. But there are also times when we stray from what we know is right. We get lost in our own concerns, suffering from the distraction of self-absorption. God recognizes this and forgives. Not only does He forgive; He forgets. Our king forgives and forgets because He is a gentle, rather than a harsh king.

Jesus is a forgiving king who desires intimacy. Heaven and hell are not distant places, but intimate realities. The kingdom—with its peace, comfort, and joy—grows within us as we grow in love through our sharing with others. You might say the kingdom involves growth into union with love, which is God. Hell, on the other hand, is separation from love. It involves feelings of rejection, shame, and loneliness. Anyone who has ever felt unloved knows what hell is. Can you imagine feeling that way forever?

Finally, God is just, but in His own way. When I meet Jesus at my end time, whenever that might be, I am convinced that He will not be the one making the final judgment; I will. After all, how could He decide my fate if He has forgotten what I've done? No, at the last judgment, I will, with God-given insight into how I have lived my life, decide between union with or separation from God, *forever*. And Jesus will accept my decision.

I don't know about you, but I prefer a God who is forgiving, intimate, and yet just. I prefer a king of unconditional love.

A king who seeks me out wherever I may be..."I myself will pasture my sheep; I will give them rest, says the Lord GOD. The lost I will seek out, the strayed I will bring back, the injured I will bind up, the sick I will heal...." (Ezekiel 34:15-16)

A king who promises new life after every ending..."In Christ shall all be brought to life...." (1 Corinthians 15:22)

A king who invites me into union with him..."Come, you who are blessed by my Father. Inherit the kingdom prepared for you from the foundation of the world." (Matthew 25:34)

I prefer this kind of God because then end times are nothing more than preludes to marvelous times of beginning anew.

1. Dennis Linn, Sheila Fabricant Linn, and Matthew Linn, *Good Goats: Healing Our Image of God*, p. 49

# Truth

Pilate was not sure of the truth. Jesus stood in front of him—a quiet man with no evidence of any royal claim. And so Pilate asked him, "Are you a king?"

Jesus answered, "Do you say this on your own, or have others told you about me?" (John 18:34)

Pilate persisted: "Then you are a king?"

Jesus made a curious response: "I came...to testify to the truth. Everyone who belongs to the truth listens to my voice." (John 18: 37)

Sometimes we are not sure of the truth. Is God really present in our lives? Is Jesus Christ real? If He is divine, shouldn't it be more obvious? Why does He seem so quiet in our lives at times, with no tangible evidence of any royal claim? And so we ask, by our actions if not our words, "Are you really a king?"

Jesus answers, "I came...to testify to the truth. Everyone who belongs to the truth listens to my voice." (John 18:37)

Is Jesus Christ real? Is Christ our King? Good questions. In my opinion, the only wrong answer is to never ask them. The search for truth is healthy. Just as physical exercise strengthens the body, so questioning strengthens our faith.

The good news is that Jesus' kingdom is based on truth. Truth means "that which is the case, even if not always recognized as such." Interestingly, truth comes from a root word that means "faithful." (1) Truth is an essential reality.

We are not forced to accept this kingdom. It is our choice. We have a gentle king, who quietly asks, "Do you say this on your own?" (John 18:34)

Truth provides fuel
for the fire called love.
Without it,
love is diminished,
often extinguished.

Truth provides balance
in the dark valleys
and bright mountaintops
of the journey
called life.

Truth is the grounding
for self-esteem

and permanence
in relationships.

The truth
sets you free.

He said,
"I am the way,
the truth
and life."

In this time
of endings
and new beginnings,
what is the truth
for you?

1. *Webster's New Collegiate Dictionary,* p. 1254

# *A Favor*

***If you have enjoyed what you have read...***

I have a favor to ask you. This book can be purchased at most on-line bookstores. Why not consider getting one for a friend or relative? And while you are at the website, please consider filling out an on-line book review. All proceeds from the sale of this book will go to charity. Besides, either or both actions will definitely help spread the word! (Pun intended.)

Yours in Christ,

Deacon Bill

# Suggested Readings

For those interested in reading more about the message of Jesus and the God He revealed, I would suggest five sources.

First, for those who grew up with an image of a judgmental and punishing God, I would highly recommend starting with *Good Goats, Healing Our Image of God* by Dennis, Sheila Fabricant and Matthew Linn (Mahwah, NJ, 1994). It is an insightful book, presented in an attractive format.

That said, the best sources for learning about Jesus are, of course, the *Gospels* themselves. At least initially, I would encourage a focus on the first three Gospels (*Matthew, Mark and Luke*), as the author of *John* assumes a familiarity with Jesus. If at all possible, read and discuss the Gospels with others. There are a variety of study guides available so a trained leader is helpful, but not necessary (entering "bible study guides" in my Internet search engine produced 238,000 entries, which means one can narrow the search to a specific bible, faith tradition or Gospel and still come up with multiple choices). I believe there are two key questions to keep in mind when discussing Gospel passages: What is the good news, and how does this relate to my life today? One of the reasons I love a discussion group approach to reading scripture is how often each participant has a different answer to these two questions.

For those who would like to know more about the historical Jesus in a highly readable book, I suggest *Jesus: A Gospel Portrait* by Donald Senior, C.P. (Mahwah, NJ, 1992). For those who would like something to reflect on each day, *Through Seasons of the Heart* by John Powell, S.J. (Allen, Texas, 1987) is an excellent book of daily meditations.

Finally, if you do not know what you want but you know you want something, try *Tuesdays with Morrie* by Mitch Albom (New York, 1997). We all have some Mitch in us, and there is a striking similarity between what Morrie has to say and what Jesus had to say. As I read the book, I couldn't help but be reminded that God always keeps His promises: just as the rain comes down, He will find a way to reach us and help us live lives that are more fruitful, if and when we are willing to absorb the gift He is trying to give us.

# Scripture Sources

Every reflection in this book began as a homily, given on some Sunday of the year. This may help explain the reason for naming a season for each reflection. The church year celebrated by most Christian faith traditions differs slightly from the calendar year, beginning in early December with Advent and ending at the end of November with the Feast of Jesus Christ the King. There is a beautiful rhythm to the church year, which is indicated under "Sunday/Feast Day" on the following page.

We Christians have inherited a three-year cycle for our Sunday and Feast Day Readings from our Jewish brothers and sisters, appropriately named Cycle A, B, and C. Every scripture quotation in this book is taken from readings in *The LECTIONARY FOR MASS, Second Typical Edition*. I am deeply indebted to the Confraternity of Christian Doctrine for their permission to use this translation of Holy Scripture.

For those who would like to reflect on the readings that gave birth to each of my reflections, the following page lists the four scripture passages for each of the Sundays involved. The first reading (usually from the Old Testament), Responsorial Psalm and Gospel deal with the same theme or themes. The Second Reading (always New Testament, with a strong focus on Paul's letters) tends to complement the main theme or themes in some way. In locating the appropriate Second Reading, a number in front of the name (e.g. 1 John) indicates which of more than one letter is the correct one. Any Second Reading that names a people rather than a person (e.g. Hebrews) is referring to one of Paul's letters.

The reader is free to use the reflections in this book in any way he or she sees fit. However, one friend has found reading the scripture passages (or at least the Gospel), followed by the reflection in this book, and then the scripture passage again a particularly effective form of meditative prayer.

| Reflection | Sunday/Feast Day | Cycle | First Reading |
|---|---|---|---|
| Repentance | Second Sunday of Advent | C | Baruch 5:1-9 |
| Belief | Fourth Sunday of Advent | A | Isaiah 7:10-14 |
| Compassion | Third Sunday of Ordinary Time | C | Nehemiah 8:2-4a,5-6,8-10 |
| Humility | Sixth Sunday of Ordinary Time | C | Jeremiah 17:5-8 |
| Hope | Eighth Sunday of Ordinary Time | A | Isaiah 49:14-15 |
| Sin | Fifth Sunday of Lent | C | Isaiah 43:16-21 |
| Forgiveness | Fourth Sunday of Lent | C | Joshua 5:9a,10-12 |
| Suffering | Palm Sunday | A | Isaiah 50:4-7 |
| Resurrection | Easter Vigil | A | Genesis 22:1-18 |
| Love | Sixth Sunday of Easter | B | Acts 10:25-26,34-35,44-48 |
| Trinity | Trinity Sunday | C | Wisdom 8:22-31 |
| Priorities | Thirteenth Sunday of Ordinary Time | A | 2 Kings 4:8-11,14-16a |
| Fear | Thirteenth Sunday of Ordinary Time | B | Wisdom 1:13-15, 2:23-24 |
| Faith | Fifteenth Sunday of Ordinary Time | A | Isaiah 55:10-11 |
| Gifts | Fifteenth Sunday of Ordinary Time | B | Amos 7:12-15 |
| Christian | Sixteenth Sunday of Ordinary Time | C | Genesis 18:1-10a |
| Kingdom | Seventeenth Sunday of Ordinary Time | A | Kings 3:5,7-12 |
| Miracles | Seventeenth Sunday of Ordinary Time | B | Kings 4:42-44 |
| Diversity | Twentieth Sunday of Ordinary Time | A | Isaiah 56:1,6-7 |
| Will Power | Twenty-Second Sunday of Ordinary Time | A | Jeremiah 20:7-9 |
| Choices | Twenty-Sixth Sunday of Ordinary Time | A | Ezekiel 18:25-28 |
| Meaning | Thirtieth Sunday of Ordinary Time | B | Jeremiah 31:7-9 |
| Salvation | Thirty-First Sunday of Ordinary Time | C | Wisdom 11:22–12:2 |
| Wisdom | Thirty-Second Sunday of Ordinary Time | A | Wisdom 6:12-16 |
| Endings | Jesus Christ The King | A | Ezekiel 34:11-12,15-17 |
| Truth | Jesus Christ the King | B | Daniel 7:13-14 |

# Sources

| Responsorial Psalm | Second Reading | Gospel |
|---|---|---|
| Ps126:1-2,2-3,4-5,6 | Philippians 1:4-6,8-11 | Luke 3:1-6 |
| Ps 24:1-2,3-4,5-6 | Romans 1:1-7 | Matthew 1:18-24 |
| Ps 19:8,9,10,15 | 1 Corinthians 12:12-30 | Luke 1:1-4, 4:14-21 |
| Ps 1:1-2,3,4 and 6 | 1 Corinthians 15:12,16-20 | Luke 6:17, 20-26 |
| Ps 62:2-3,6-7,8-9 | 1 Corinthians 4:1-5 | Matthew 6:24-34 |
| Ps 126:1-2,2-3,4-5,6 | Philippians 3:8-14 | John 8:1-11 |
| Ps 34:2-3,4-5,6-7 | 2 Corinthians 5:17-21 | Luke 15:1-3,11-32 |
| Ps 22:8-9,17-18,19-20,23-24 | Philippians 2:6-11 | Matthew 26:14-27:66 |
| Ps16:5,8,9-10,11 | Romans 6:3-11 | Matthew 28:1-10 |
| Ps 98:1,2-3,3,4 | 1 John 4:7-10 | John 15:9-17 |
| Ps 8:4-5,6-7,8-9 | Romans 5:1-5 | John 16:12-15 |
| Ps 89:2-3,16-17,18-19 | Romans 6:3-4,8-11 | Matthew 10:37-42 |
| Ps 30:2,4,5-6,11,12,13 | 2 Corinthians 8:7,9,13-15 | Mark 5:21-43 |
| Ps 65:10,11,12-13,14 | Romans 8:18-23 | Matthew 13:1-9 |
| Ps 85:9-10,11-12,13-14 | Ephesians 1:3-10 | Mark 6:7-13 |
| Ps 15:2-3,3-4,5 | Colossians 1:24-28 | Luke 10:38-42 |
| Ps 119:57,72,76-77,127-128,129-130 | Romans 8:28-30 | Matthew 13:44-46 |
| Ps 145:10-11,15-16,17-18 | Ephesians 4:1-6 | John 6:1-15 |
| Ps 67:2-3,5,6,8 | Romans 11:13-15,29-32 | Matthew 15:21-28 |
| Ps 63:2,3-4,5-6,8-9 | Romans 12:1-2 | Matthew 16:21-27 |
| Ps 25:4-5,6-7,8-9 | Philippians 2:1-5 | Matthew 21:28-32 |
| Ps 126:1-2,2-3,4-5,6 | Hebrews 5:1-6 | Mark 10:46-52 |
| Ps 145:1-2,8-9,10-11,13,14 | 2 Thessalonians 1:11–2:2 | Luke 19:1-10 |
| Ps 63:2,3-4,5-6,7-8 | 1 Thessalonians 4:13-18 | Matthew 25:1-13 |
| Ps 23:1-2,2-3,5-6 | 1 Corinthians 15:20-26,28 | Matthew 25:31-46 |
| Ps 93:1,1-2,5 | Book of Revelation 1:5-8 | John 1:5-8 |

0-595-33164-5

Printed in the United States
23210LVS00002B/88-720